COMPASSION BASED RECOVERY

*Healing from addiction
with compassion & curiosity*

NICHOLE SLOAN LCSW

To request permissions, contact the publisher at
compassionbasedrecovery@gmail.com

Paperback: 979-8-218-33051-4
Ebook: 979-8-218-33824-4

First paperback edition December 2023

Written & Edited by Nichole Sloan
Cover art by Wycinanki Polish Folk Art
Layout by Henrietta Sampson

Printed by Compassion Based Recovery in the USA.

CompassionBasedRecovery.com

Dedication

To the collective consciousness of love, the interconnected web
of all that is, may I stay in reverence.

To all of the ancestors and teachers, may I remain in humble
gratitude for all of the wisdom remembered, explored, and shared.

To all of my loved ones, you've kept me feeling loved, seen, and
heard, and for this, I am forever grateful.

May you always know how much you are loved.

May all beings be happy.

May all beings be free from suffering and the causes of suffering.

May we all remember how sacred it is to be alive at all.

Life is an altar, every action an offering.

Table of Contents

WELCOME!

"In the end, only three things matter: how much
you loved, how gently you lived, and how gracefully
you let go of things not meant for you."

Buddha

I want to first commend you for taking this step towards well-being for yourself. It is such a brave step to start the process of healing and recovery. Addiction can be a severe and dangerous disease. Depending on the substance you use and the level of your use, it may be advisable to consult a healthcare professional at the start of your journey. They can help you create a personalized treatment plan and offer medical assistance if needed.

The fact that you chose to acknowledge that you could benefit from taking better care of yourself or that you planted the seed of wanting to heal is so important and powerful!

So, as we begin, take a moment to give yourself some kindness, some praise, some kudos, and some acknowledgment that the step you're taking requires bravery and self-love!

I'd like you to repeat these compassionate statements to yourself and see how they feel in your mind and body.

I am worthy. I am worthy of love. I am worthy of love simply because I exist. I am worthy of forgiveness. I am capable of healing. I am brave. It is okay not to be perfect; no one is. I am a work in progress. I am lovable. When I know better, I do better. I am slowly making patient progress. It is brave of me to work on my recovery. It is brave of me to step outside of my comfort zone. It is brave of me to take my healing into my own hands. It is brave of me to start to look at the things I've pushed away for so long. I am capable of change. I am capable of learning to love myself.

Those are just a few compassionate statements: how did it feel in your body? You may have felt peace or reassurance, or maybe you felt pushback, and it felt icky. Both are okay. It just shows you where you are in your journey to compassion.

Throughout this workbook, I will use compassion as a lens to look at your recovery process. Why compassion? After years of working in addiction and recovery, the most significant contributor to continued drug and alcohol use or relapse that I've seen has been shame, guilt, regret, and anger toward self. Rarely do these painful emotions alone lead to long-term recovery. I believe compassion towards self and others lead to long-term sobriety and a sense of happiness in life.

I will also use poems, stories, and metaphors to help illustrate the recovery process. A story or an image can paint a picture or explain a concept more easily. I've tried to make some of the metaphors fun!

Each section of the workbook will have a place for compassionate reflection. These blank spaces are the most important part of the entire workbook. I will offer knowledge and questions for reflection, however;

Your words to yourself will be the most healing and the most powerful.

When you reach the parts of the workbook for compassionate reflection, grab a pen and sit quietly for a few minutes. Reflect on the questions and see what comes up for you in your heart and your mind. You are the architect of your own life.

You are the expert on your own life.

Your ever-present wisdom will start to come through the more you sit and reflect on what is most needed for you at this time in your life.

I encourage you to use this workbook honestly and openly with yourself to allow yourself to take an honest inventory of what is going on with you both inside and outside of your life.

Some topics we explore may be complex or challenging, but remember, as we move through this process, that you are worthy of healing, love, and self-love and capable of being an agent of change in your life.

THE WHY:

Why do you want to stop using substances?

"A person often meets his destiny on
the road he took to avoid it."

Jean de la Fontaine

You bought this book for a reason, and I want to ask, "Why?"—your WHY is very important. Take a moment to reflect. What are the reasons that you want to recover?

Maybe it is because you want to feel better physically, mentally, and emotionally. Maybe it is because you know you are capable of much more. Maybe that's because you want to develop deeper and more meaningful relationships with yourself and others.

Remembering your WHY can be an essential tool when you're having a difficult day in your recovery, when you feel like using substances, saying f-it, or you don't remember the reasons you started your journey in the first place.

Writing down the reasons you want to change can be a reminder in times of difficulty and be a helpful, motivating tool.

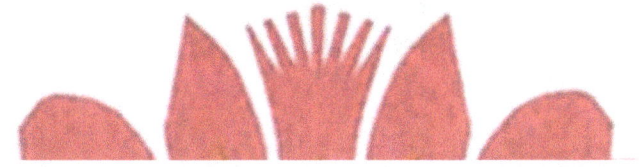

Compassionate Reflection

I'd like you to take a moment to reflect on why you chose to work on your recovery.

Ex. I have dreams of a bigger life; I want to be happier, I want to be a better parent or partner, I want to feel more peace, I am sick and tired of feeling sick and tired, I want to feel clever and witty again.

_____

_____

_____

_____

_____

_____

_____

_____

_____

_____

_____

_____

_____

_____

_____

_____

_____

In moments of difficulty, it can be helpful to remember your WHY.

THE WHY:

Why did you use substances?

"I drank to drown my sorrows, but the damned things learned how to swim."

Frida Kahlo

You used substances for a reason. Yes, sometimes it was to feel high or just to have a good time. Maybe it started that way. But for most people reading this workbook, you've likely been using substances more and more, with increased tolerance and increased consequences both physically, emotionally, and spiritually.

However, it's okay to admit that substances worked and helped with some parts of your life for a long time until they didn't.

Please explore how the substances helped you. For some people, the reason may be that substances helped them to deal with their difficult emotions, to be able to go to sleep, to manage social anxiety, to manage unhealed trauma, to numb out, to manage depression, to feel happiness, to fit in with their friends, etc.

Each person's reasons will be different. So, take a minute below and list why you used substances and what parts of your life the substances helped you to manage.

Compassionate Reflection

WHY did you use substances? How did they benefit you?

Ex. I used alcohol to feel happiness when I was so depressed; Cocaine helped me to laugh for a while and forget how miserable I was. I smoked marijuana to manage my anxiety, and I drank to deal with my PTSD nightmares and to fall asleep.

Why do we make this list?

Because the reasons you used will become your goals in recovery.

Meaning that if you always used substances to fall asleep, sleep hygiene will be essential in your recovery. If you used substances to deal with your trauma and the complex emotions that came up with it, healing your trauma will be an important part of your recovery. If you use substances to manage your anxiety or depression, managing your anxiety or depression will become an essential part of your recovery.

Have compassion for yourself that no one says when they're a child - I want to grow up and be an addict or an alcoholic. No one, when coming up with their life goals, says - I hope that I have to go into treatment, and I hope that I have to read a workbook to learn to better manage my substance use. No one chooses this. However, there is a reason that you are here.

There is a reason that you became addicted. And more often than not, *that reason is very painful.* So, with compassion, offer yourself some kindness that you used because you didn't know what else to do to manage your experience. If you had known another way, you wouldn't have chosen to use substances over and over. You didn't know that you would get so addicted.

Can you take a few minutes and offer yourself some compassion and kindness that you were doing the best you could with what you had at the time and you were using substances to deal with some very difficult experiences?

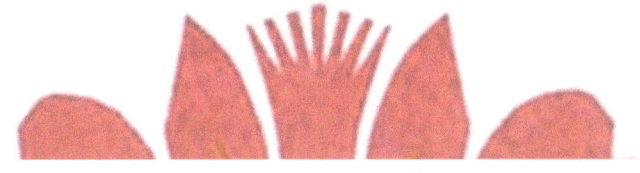

Compassionate Reflection

What kindness can you offer yourself as you think about the reasons you used?

Ex. I used to drink because I was so anxious, and I didn't know how to relax sober. It's difficult for me to feel comfortable and safe in my body. I had no idea that my drinking would become such an issue. I may really need support around my anxiety, maybe even a therapist.

YOUR TOOLBOX

"Still, I rise."

Maya Angelou

Each of us has a unique set of skills and tools we've developed, some out of survival, some out of necessity, and some just because we are unique. I'd like you to reflect on what skills you bring to your life that I've helped you survive and have helped you in times of great difficulty.

What are your internal strengths? Take a moment and explore what skills you have that are unique to you.

You may be resilient, funny, clever, creative, smart, persistent, logical, curious, determined, or kind towards others. The traits and skills are endless!

Remember, recovery is a unique journey; what works for one person may not work for another. Experimenting with different coping skills and strategies to find what resonates with you and supports your recovery goals is essential. Seeking professional guidance from therapists, counselors, or support groups can also provide valuable assistance during the recovery process.

Please take a moment and explore what you have in your toolbox that helps you manage all that life throws at you in your day-to-day life.

Compassionate Reflection

What are your strengths?

Ex. I am so smart! I am funny! I'm a good friend! I am a survivor! I am kind! I have good insight on what is going on with me! I am loyal! I am loving!

The first metaphor that I want you to think about is a toolbox. You have some tools you've already developed throughout your life in your toolbox.

Throughout this workbook, we are going to add tools to your toolbox. Developing a toolbox is essential because, as you know, nothing can be built without tools. An empty toolbox will only get you so far as you move through life. Neither will a toolbox with only one tool. You can't build a house with only one hammer. You will need a variety of tools for your journey of recovery.

Deciding what tools work best for you will be necessary. Some of the tools we go through in this book will resonate with you, and others you will find unhelpful. That is okay.

Take the tools that work for you and leave the rest.

Compassionate Reflection

What tools have helped you in your life so far?

Ex. Street smarts, resilience, humor, intelligence, big heart.

_____

_____

_____

_____

_____

_____

What tools are you interested in adding to your toolbox? Or what problems are you experiencing that you need a tool for?

Ex. I want to start group therapy, I can watch more funny shows when I'm upset, and I can start meditating. I'm unsure of what to do when I'm having a craving or when I'm really angry, so I will need a tool for that.

_____

_____

_____

_____

_____

_____

_____

WHAT IS COMPASSION?

"And I said to my body softly, 'I want to be
your friend.' It took a long breath and replied,
'I have been waiting my whole life for this.'"

Nayyirah Waheed

This workbook is entitled Compassion-Based Recovery, so it only makes sense to start talking about compassion.

Compassion has many definitions, but I can start with my favorite, which comes from Cognitively-Based Compassion Training (CBCT®):

"Compassion is the warm-hearted concern that unfolds when we witness the suffering of others and feel motivated to relieve it."

With Compassion-Based Recovery (CBR), we meet the present suffering (the addiction) with kindness and warmth. We feel motivated to actively engage in a journey of recovery. We continue to meet our experiences with curiosity and compassion. We explore compassionately the reasons you became addicted and how it has affected your life and your relationships. We learn to be mindful of our experiences, the good, the neutral, and the difficult. We explore how to compassionately manage emotions, explore our thinking, and manage our cravings in recovery. And we learn how to love ourselves, one moment at a time.

Compassion is a verb, just as recovery is a verb. It asks us to take action to relieve our suffering and the suffering of others.

A compassionate recovery does not just happen to you; you must actively build your own compassionate road to recovery.

In this workbook, we also work with self-compassion. Below is one definition of self-compassion which comes from the work of Kristen Neff:

"Self-compassion has been defined as a self-attitude that involves treating oneself with warmth and understanding in difficult times and recognizing that making mistakes is part of being human." [1]

By using the lens of self-compassion, we can acknowledge and explore how part of being human is inevitably making mistakes. We can then learn to meet our mistakes with a mindful and compassionate lens, allowing the mistakes not to define us but to teach us and guide us toward long-term recovery.

Sometimes, it can be helpful to explore compassion by exploring the opposite of compassion- harshness.

So often, in addiction, there is an overwhelming amount of harshness, shame, regret, sadness, and overall suffering. And so often, people, for many years, will try and stop using substances by shaming themselves into abstinence or sobriety. This is sometimes referred to as "tough love." And as you know, shame or harshness is not enough to become sober. Self-hate is not enough to become sober. Burning your life to the ground is not enough to become sober. Harshness often only creates more feelings of shame and low self-worth; it rarely motivates us to engage in recovery.

So often, many have tried to use harshness to end addiction to no avail. Throughout this workbook, instead of harshness, we will begin to use the skills of kindness, self-love, self-care, rethinking, curious exploration, acceptance, mindfulness, and compassion to treat the addiction and to heal.

---

1 (Neff, 2003)." (Breines & Chen, 2012).
    Breines, J. G., & Chen, S. (2012). Self-Compassion Increases Self-Improvement Motivation. *Society for Personality and Social Psychology, 38* (9), 1133-1143.

31

We will find that when we meet addiction and suffering with mindfulness and compassion, we can have increased clarity and perspective, self-love and self-acceptance, feel more connected to the web of humanity, and be better prepared to engage in a transformative, healing, and compassionate journey to recovery.

Compassion allows for us to hold our experiences in a certain way. It allows for a gentle holding of the self, which allows for healing, transformation, and serenity. Throughout this workbook, we will examine our experiences through a compassionate lens.

Compassion is an essential tool for long-term recovery.

Compassionate Reflection

How have you used harshness to stop using? How have you talked harshly to yourself?

Ex. Almost every day, I say something critical or mean to myself; I've been talking to myself this way since I was a teenager. I try and use tough love on myself to get myself not to drink but it never works. I tell myself things like: I've turned into such a loser; I can't just have one drink like everyone else; I'm not normal, I'm weak, and I have no willpower; I'm crazy.

_____

_____

_____

_____

_____

_____

_____

_____

_____

_____

_____

_____

_____

_____

_____

_____

_____

Do you experience any shame, regret, or anger towards yourself when you think about your addiction?

Ex. I feel so ashamed over how I yelled at my girlfriend and didn't even remember it; I don't like the example I'm setting for my kids. I'm so embarrassed about how I spend most of my days getting high and ignoring calls from my family and friends.

_____

_____

_____

_____

_____

_____

_____

_____

_____

_____

_____

_____

_____

_____

_____

_____

_____

_____

_____

_____

Is compassion comfortable or uncomfortable for you? Do you know how to offer yourself compassion?

Ex. I am my worst enemy; I am always putting myself down and being critical of myself. Being compassionate feels lame and like I'm giving myself the easy way out, it's totally uncomfortable. I honestly don't have any idea how to be compassionate towards myself, especially about my substance use.

_____

_____

_____

_____

_____

_____

_____

What is your initial reaction when being asked to use compassion to heal?

Ex. This is cheesy or sappy; this is some hippie stuff; if I'm too nice to myself, I'll never stop. To be honest, I'm not really sure that being kind to myself will help me to change anything.

_____

_____

_____

_____

_____

_____

COMPASSIONATE CURIOSITY

"The doors to the world of the wild Self are few but precious. If you have a deep scar, that is a door, if you have an old, old story, that is a door. If you love the sky and the water so much you almost cannot bear it, that is a door. If you yearn for a deeper life, a full life, a sane life, that is a door."

Clarissa Pinkola Estés

You are not something that needs to be fixed; you are not broken

You are having a moment of difficulty, and we can work on learning how to best love ourselves with curiosity and compassion. We can learn how to navigate life's ups and downs and life's seasons with compassion and curiosity. None of us are perfect, and everyone makes mistakes and experiences suffering. Instead of fixing you, we will learn how to *manage* your experiences with compassion.

One tool that I would like to help you develop is compassionate curiosity.

I'd like for you to meet yourself with an investigative lens. Start to have some curiosity as to what triggers you, what led you to addiction, and also what kept you in addiction.

I encourage you to be curious about how you talk to yourself, meet your emotions, and how much energy you put into your healing and recovery.

For many people, what will come up when we ask those questions will be a lot of self-criticism and shame, and the "could've, should've, and would've's." The "I should've done things differently" and "I could've done things differently."

Yes, you could have. However, that line of thinking is often not helpful and results in more shame, more guilt, and more sadness, which ultimately leads to more substance use.

So, instead, I'd like to be curious about the whys. Get to the root of the issue, not just the surface issues.

Once we explore the WHY, we can meet the answers that come up with compassion. Compassion for the child who suffered and compassion for the teenager who didn't know better when they picked up that first joint or drink. Having compassion for the adult that has so much trauma and has had so many negative life experiences, and the only way they knew how to cope was through substance use or suppressing their emotions. Having compassion that surviving this life is very difficult, and you did your best with what you had at that time.

As we move through this and you notice that shame, guilt, or negative self-talk comes up, pause for a moment and ask yourself,

Can I meet this moment with Compassion?

Ask yourself, does my self-criticism make things better or worse? Can I explore with curiosity, with an investigative lens as to why and how I got here? Have compassion over how hard it was for you to go through those experiences and how hard it has been for you to stay stuck in addiction.

Compassion is not the same as permission.

Having compassion for ourselves does not give us a pass to do or say whatever we want. Compassion offers a lens through which we can look at our experience with a little more kindness so that, ultimately, when we're kind and loving, we will be more honest with ourselves.

The more honest our inventory of ourselves, the more capable we are of making deliberate and conscious decisions to change and grow. Consequently, we will be more motivated to make changes that align with a version of ourselves that is the most loved and cared for, resilient and ever-growing.

Compassionate Reflection

What part of your addiction is the hardest for you to explore compassionately?

Ex. I have a tough time forgiving myself for being such a jerk when I drink; I have a hard time being okay with the fact I go AWOL for days and ignore calls when I'm high.

_____

_____

_____

_____

_____

_____

_____

At what age did you start using substances? What age were you when you became addicted?

Ex. I started experimenting at age 14 but I didn't get addicted and use regularly until my early 30s.

_____

_____

_____

_____

_____

What were you going through when you became the most addicted?

Ex. I think I probably had depression and didn't know it; I was going through my first divorce, I didn't know what to do with my life, my childhood sexual abuse kept coming up, and I didn't know how to cope with it.

_____

_____

_____

_____

_____

_____

_____

_____

_____

_____

_____

_____

_____

_____

_____

_____

_____

_____

_____

TO BE HONEST

"Vulnerability is our most accurate
measurement of courage."

Brené Brown

Addiction thrives in dishonesty. Dishonesty towards self and dishonesty towards others. A willingness to engage in compassionate honesty is required to heal and to recover. To fully recover, we first must be willing to take an honest inventory of all the things we lied about.

Let's start with having compassion for ourselves that you lied because the truth was so uncomfortable.

Honesty does not mean what I lied about was okay or acceptable. *What it does mean is that you lied for a reason.*

Likely, you lied to keep the addiction alive or because you didn't know how else to manage your experiences or emotions.

You lied because the truth was too painful. You lied because you didn't know how others would respond to your truth. You lied because the shame was so heavy.

In addiction, we lie about so much: how much we used, when we used, where we were, who we were with, how much money we spent, how we are feeling, what traumas we have been through, and how they impacted us, our fears, what we did and why.

Addiction loves dishonesty because it keeps the addiction fed.

One of the biggest lies people tell themselves is that they are social users or that they are not addicted. Take a moment and reflect if your use has become out of control.

Ask yourself if your use has negatively impacted your quality of life. Ask yourself if you've tried to stop and have been unable to. Be honest about the extent of your addiction and the harm it has caused you.

You're not a bad person for having lied. However, now is an opportunity to start being honest about what you lied about and why.

We cannot change what we do not acknowledge.

Compassionate Reflection

What did you lie about in your addiction? To yourself or others?

Ex. I lied about how much I used, when I used, where I went, who I was with, how much money I spent, how I am feeling, what I did or why; I've even lied to myself that I am addicted.

_____

_____

_____

_____

_____

_____

_____

_____

_____

_____

_____

_____

_____

_____

_____

_____

_____

_____

_____

_____

What emotions come up when you think about being honest with yourself? With others?

Ex. I'm terrified that others won't understand that I lied about drinking because I didn't know how else to cope with my depression and fit in. I lie to myself that I'm addicted, and I'm scared to admit to myself that I may not be able to get high anymore. I'm so embarrassed that lying comes so easily for me now.

_____

_____

_____

_____

_____

_____

_____

_____

_____

_____

_____

_____

_____

_____

_____

_____

_____

BELOW THE STORM

"You are the sky.
Everything else – it's just the weather."

Pema Chödrön

I want you to imagine the image of an ocean with a terrible hurricane or storm on the surface. Imagine large waves crashing, horrible lightning, and thunder. Now, please start to go below the surface 10 feet, 100 feet, and 1000 feet, and imagine the stillness there.

Both the stillness and the storm can exist at the same time.

Taking a moment and being still can be helpful in moments of emotional storm or intensity. There are many tools that we can use to be still. One tool that I strongly recommend is meditation and mindfulness. For those of you who aren't aware, mindfulness, as defined by Jon Kabat Zinn, the founder of Mindfulness-Based Stress Reduction, is the skill of:

Paying attention to the present moment, on purpose and non-judgmentally

Mindfulness is a helpful tool for us to start to become aware of what is happening in our lives at THIS very moment.

So often, our mind is preoccupied with the past, traumas, regrets, and things we wish we would have done. Or our mind goes to the future, to our never-ending list of worries, what could go wrong or worst-case scenario thinking, and the never-ending list of adulting.

What often happens when we let our mind go on autopilot to the past and then the future is we find ourselves, like a ping pong ball, going back and forth between depression or anxiety, depression, or anxiety. And so often, when we're stuck in the cycle, we don't notice the present moment, the only moment of power in our lives.

The present moment is where our lives take place; if we miss this, we miss our very lives.

We miss our moment of power to make change and heal in our own lives. The first step in any mindfulness practice is focusing the mind on one point of attention, stilling the mind in the present moment.

This can be hard for some people who have experienced trauma or have been addicted for a long time. Being still, physically or mentally, doesn't always feel safe, and it can feel very uncomfortable. So, it's okay if you start with just a few minutes or even if it's just a few seconds. Beginning with mindful movement or a walking mindfulness meditation can also be very helpful if being still is hard for you.

If you are able to engage in a sitting meditation, I recommend finding a comfortable position. Notice your posture; have your back upright but not uptight and the belly soft. Start by bringing your awareness to your breath. Notice the inhalation, the exhalation, and the brief pause in between, and explore to see if you can bring awareness to the breath of THIS moment. Spend a moment and observe the breath. Don't try to breathe slow or deep; in fact, let go of control of the breath and allow the body to breathe itself. Just witness and observe the breath.

The mind is going to wander because that's what minds do. So, try not going to judge yourself for where your mind goes. Beginner meditator's minds are often called "puppy minds" because it's like putting a puppy in a room of squirrels and telling it to sit. (It won't; it excitedly goes after every squirrel, which is what our minds do; they follow every thought!)

As we practice mindfulness, we will notice when the mind strays away; then, we can bring our attention back to the breath. Mindfulness if not preventing thoughts or being all zen'ed out. Mindfulness is not floating in space and not thinking about anything. Mindfulness is noticing when the mind wanders and bringing it back to your anchor to the present moment. See if you can practice this for sixty seconds or even three minutes!

Explore as you become mentally and physically still if you experience the present moment more clearly.

Many helpful websites have a lot of very high-quality meditations that can help you to still the mind in the present moment. Simply turning to the internet for "mindfulness meditations" can be very useful.

I highly recommend taking an 8-week mindfulness course such as Mindfulness-Based Stress Reduction (MBSR) or a compassion-based course such as Cognitively Based Compassion Training (CBCT) or Mindful Self Compassion (MSC). These courses will offer you clear instructions on how to begin a mindfulness and compassion practice of your own.

Here are some of the key benefits associated with a regular mindfulness practice: Stress reduction, improved ability to regulate emotions, better focus and concentration, better self-awareness, better cognitive functioning, improved sleep quality, pain management, improved well-being and relationships, reduced symptoms of anxiety and depression and lower blood pressure.

Studies have shown that if you practice meditation for 15 minutes a day for eight weeks, some structures in the brain begin to change. So not only will mindfulness practice help you to become more aware of your own life in the present moment and your stillness below the surface, it can also have many additional benefits as listed above.

For a lot of people, when they first start to meditate or to become aware of the present moment, they notice that their mind is a bad neighborhood; they see there are a lot of thoughts and memories in their mind that they try to avoid, they notice that their thoughts are constantly racing, and I want just to let you know this is entirely normal.

Before we can start working with the mind, we first have to be able to witness it and see what's going on there. This can be hard for people - becoming aware of the racing thoughts, the cravings to use substances, the constant anxiety, the worry, grief, or depression.

Trust me, eventually, as you get to know yourself and your mind better, you will learn that *you are not your thoughts*.

Throughout this workbook, we will learn how to work with our thoughts, how to work with our emotions, and how to find stillness even in the face of a storm.

Compassionate Reflection

Try practicing one mindfulness meditation today. I'd recommend doing a "body scan" or a "mindfulness of breathing" meditation. See what it feels like to be mindful of the present moment. What was this exercise like for you?

Ex. My mind kept racing; concentrating was hard; I felt tired and peaceful afterward.

_____

_____

_____

_____

_____

What comes up for you when you bring your attention to your thoughts?

Ex. I think a lot about the same topics; I stay focused on how I'm going to be able to stay sober forever, I talk mean to myself, and I always go to what I'm worried about

_____

_____

_____

_____

_____

Another tool, paying attention to our senses, can help us return to the present moment and find stillness. Let's take a moment and engage in a grounding exercise from Dialectical Behavioral Therapy, "DBT," called 5-4-3-2-1.

The DBT 5-4-3-2-1 exercise is a grounding technique often used in Dialectical Behavior Therapy (DBT), a form of cognitive-behavioral therapy developed by Dr. Marsha Linehan. This exercise is designed to help individuals become more aware of their surroundings and bring their attention to the present moment, especially during times of heightened emotional distress or anxiety. The numbers 5, 4, 3, 2, and 1 correspond to a sequence of steps to guide individuals through the process of grounding themselves.

Here's how it typically works:

1. 5 Things You Can See:
   - Look around and identify five things you can see in your immediate environment. It could be anything from objects in the room to colors, shapes, or patterns. You can choose to look for five things that are the same color, for example.

2. 4 Things You Can Touch:
   - Identify four things you can touch or feel in your environment. Try and feel four different textures. It might be the texture of your clothes, the surface of a table, or the feeling of the air on your skin.

3. 3 Things You Can Hear:
   - Listen for three distinct sounds in your surroundings. It could be the hum of a computer, birds chirping outside, or the sound of footsteps.

4. 2 Things You Can Smell:
   - Identify two smells in your environment. This could be the scent of a nearby plant, food, or your perfume.

5. 1 Thing You Can Taste:

- Finally, pay attention to your sense of taste. Identify one thing you can taste, even if it's just your morning breath!

By going through these steps, you will start to engage your senses and redirect your attention to the present moment. This grounding exercise is beneficial when you feel overwhelmed, anxious, or dissociated. It helps bring awareness back to the immediate surroundings, promoting a sense of calm and present moment awareness.

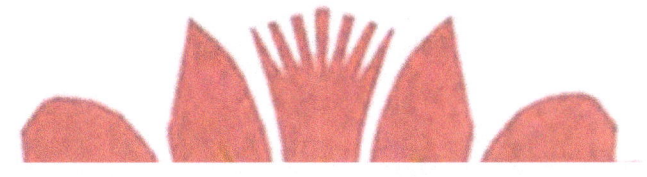

Compassionate Reflection

What parts of your life do you miss when you are on autopilot or "zoned out"?

Ex. I miss what my kids are saying or doing all of the time; my partner always asks if I'm listening, I miss essential instructions on the job site, and I get lost driving home sometimes.

_____

_____

_____

_____

_____

_____

_____

_____

_____

_____

_____

_____

_____

_____

_____

_____

_____

_____

_____

Another tool you can use for stillness is music. I highly encourage people to listen to healing frequencies. If you search online for 'healing frequencies,' you will find many. For many, this is often thought of as relaxation or spa music. Healing frequencies are often associated with alternative and complementary medicine, particularly sound therapy and vibrational medicine.

Any music, whether it be classical, jazz or healing frequencies can help you to be mentally still, allowing you to then be physically still. The more we allow ourselves to be still, both mentally and physically, the more we can examine what is happening to us in the present moment.

Often, our healing lies below the surface.

Often, our healing lies in what we *don't* talk about.

Often, our healing lies in what keeps us up at night. As we become still, we can start to explore where our healing lies.

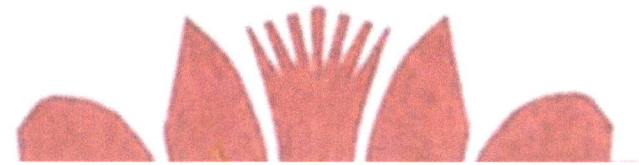

Compassionate Reflection

What keeps you up at night? Or what do you avoid thinking or talking about? This is where the healing lies, most likely.

Ex. I was abused as a kid, and I never told anyone; my combat PTSD still haunts me, and I don't know where to start to heal it. I'm so lonely and have no idea how to make friends; I'm sad every day, and it's hard to get out of bed most days.

_____

_____

_____

_____

_____

_____

_____

What was it like to bring your awareness to the present moment?

Ex. I realized I'm never fully present; I'm always in the past or future. I realized my mind moves fast.

_____

_____

_____

_____

YOUR GARDEN

"When a flower doesn't bloom you fix the environment in which it grows, not the flower."

Alexander Den Heijer

Recovery is a process; I think of it as a garden. For any of you who have spent time in a garden or grown anything from a house plant to a potato that you left too long on the counter, and it grew roots… We have an understanding that, in nature, things take time. There is no immediate growth, and everything takes its natural time.

You are no different.

I'd like for you to start by thinking of your recovery as a garden. The seeds you are planting today may take weeks or months to sprout. Plant anyway.

If we want to start a garden, the first thing we need to do is till the soil and clear it of anything that could harm the plants or the seeds we are planting. We remove weeds and pests and prepare the ground for planting.

So, please take a moment and review what it is in your life that you need to remove from your soil. Think about the people, places, and things in your life that are toxic to you, cause harm, or do not enable your growth.

Explore what people you used to use substances with or that encouraged you to use. Explore what people treat you poorly or are abusive to you.

Explore what places you used to use substances at, the neighborhoods or houses where you used to buy substances, and the corner store or bar where you used to get drinks.

Explore what things you need to remove, such as your drug paraphernalia, your liquor cabinet, or your posters of substance use.

Identifying the people, places, and things harmful to your recovery will ultimately help to make your recovery garden thrive.

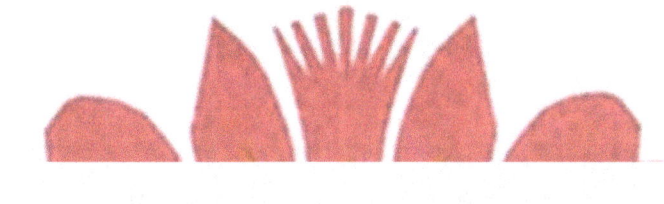

Compassionate Reflection

What people may I need to remove from my life? And how are they risky to your recovery or healing?

Ex. My friends from the bar, my abusive ex, my dealer. I love my friends, but they always encourage me to use and say it's no big deal, they really put my sobriety at risk.

_____

_____

_____

_____

How does that make you feel?

Ex. I'm terrified if I remove everyone who is toxic, I'll have no one; all my friends drink, and I'm so scared of having to start over.

_____

_____

_____

_____

_____

_____

_____

_____

Creating distance from people who are actively using can be difficult. Have compassion for yourself, knowing that you will miss people and love people who are unhealthy for you.

Have patience and kindness for yourself. It can be sad to let go of people that you love deeply but that you know are stuck in their addiction or are emotionally or physically abusive to you.

I know that creating new relationships can be difficult and sometimes scary, so have patience with yourself as you learn to connect with people in a sober way and develop new relationships.

One great place to develop sober relationships is through recovery meetings, such as Alcoholics Anonymous (AA) or Narcotics Anonymous (NA). There are also SMART recovery meetings (science-based and non-religious), as well as Buddhist recovery meetings. Also, getting reconnected to old or new hobbies and interests can be a great place to meet new people.

Just know it's normal to grieve the loss of relationships of people that you love but that you know are also in active addiction.

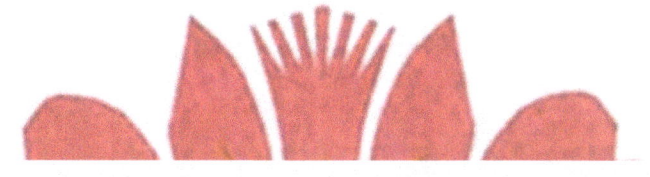

Compassionate Reflection

What kindness can you offer yourself as you undergo this change in your relationships?

Ex. I made friends in my twenties by going to hobbies I liked, and I can do that again. I'm a pretty interesting person, and I can try to start conversations with coworkers or reconnect with old friends; it's okay that I feel uncomfortable making new friends. A lot of people have social anxiety, and it's normal to feel overwhelmed when making significant life changes.

What words of comfort can you offer yourself for the loss you are experiencing by letting go of some relationships?

Ex. I'm so sad letting go of the only friend I've had for a long time; even though he is my dealer, he's also looked out for me during some hard times. I can offer myself a break that losing people might make me sad, and that's okay.

_____
_____
_____
_____
_____
_____
_____
_____
_____
_____
_____
_____
_____
_____
_____
_____
_____
_____
_____
_____

What places do I need to stop going to that are risky to my recovery?

Ex. The bar, the football game, the 420 festivals, my own she-shed or man cave.

_____

_____

_____

_____

_____

_____

_____

What things do I need to remove from my life?

Ex. Remove all substances and paraphernalia from the house, delete my dealer's number, delete my abusive ex's number, or block them.

_____

_____

_____

_____

_____

_____

_____

YOUR SEEDS

"The day you plant the seed is not
the day you eat the fruit."

Fabienne Fredrickson

Once we clear the soil of all the pests and the weeds, we can plant our seeds. Take a moment and explore what seeds you want to plant.

Maybe this is a seed of happiness, maybe this is a seed of sobriety, maybe this is a seed of self-love, but take a moment and think, what is it that I want to plant? What are the goals you are working towards today?

Please think about nature and how after we plant something, it doesn't grow right away. You are no different than nature, and the seeds within you that you are planting will also take time to grow.

You will have seasons where there is lots of growth (like Spring and Summer), you will have seasons where it feels like nothing is changing (like Winter), you will have seasons where there is some growth and some destruction (like Fall). And all of this is natural to be expected.

What is important is to start to recognize that change takes time, recovery takes time, and growth takes time. Often, in addiction, we are used to immediate gratification. You're having a difficult day; you hit a blunt, feel better immediately, and have immediate gratification. You're having a difficult experience; you drink a pint and feel better immediately. So, the addicted brain gets used to having immediate gratification. The addicted brain craves and expects immediate gratification.

One of the hard things to get used to in recovery is that sometimes we must sit with discomfort for longer than we would like. Sitting in the "grey," the unknown, the uncomfortable, or the unresolved can be initially be hugely uncomfortable.

We must have patience with the growing process within ourselves. Start by creating space in your mind that *this recovery process will take as much time as it needs*. Start to acknowledge what feelings come up internally when

I face the reality that my healing will take time. This may be feelings of impatience, frustration, irritability… Explore within yourself what feelings come up when you think your recovery may take days, months, or years.

Compassionate Reflection

What seeds am I planting? (What are my goals, hopes, and dreams)

Ex. I want to get back in shape; I want to learn how to cook; I want to be happy; I want to go to therapy; I want to travel, and I want to be SOBER!

_____
_____
_____
_____
_____
_____
_____
_____
_____
_____
_____
_____
_____
_____
_____
_____
_____
_____
_____
_____

What comes up when you think about how your healing may take time?

Ex. I'm overwhelmed, I don't believe I'm going to be able to stay sober, I'm unsure if I can make my dreams come true, and I'm also low-key excited to start.

_____

_____

_____

_____

_____

_____

_____

_____

_____

_____

_____

_____

_____

_____

_____

_____

_____

_____

_____

_____

THE DIAGNOSTIC

"Until you make the unconscious conscious,
it will direct your life and you will call it fate."

C.G. Jung

Addiction is sometimes called a feeling disease because we use substances to deal with our emotions. Learning to manage our emotions becomes an essential tool in recovery. We can start by recognizing the very complex internal landscape of emotions.

Emotions are often scary and difficult for people, so people spend a lot of time running from emotions or trying to push them away or avoid them entirely by numbing themselves.

Throughout this workbook, we will work on developing a vocabulary of emotions and a better understanding of our internal emotional landscape and how to manage them.

The first part of learning to work with your emotions is to be able to name them and identify them. *We name it to tame it!* This is much like when we take our car to the shop to get fixed.

The mechanic will run a diagnostic. Why do they do that? To find the problem and fix it, right? We wouldn't trust a mechanic who just guessed what the problem was. We are just the same as the car; we need to run a diagnostic on our emotional experiences in order to know how to manage them!

Anytime we have an intense emotion, it's important to identify and name it. I always say- name it to tame it! The reason is that the tools we use for anger will differ from those we use for sadness. The tools we use for grief or shame will be different than the tools we use for fear.

Just like we can't build a house with just one hammer, we will need many tools to deal with our emotional experiences.

The first tool that I want to offer you is the feeling wheel. It gives you the language to name and work with your emotions. The different basic emotions are in the center that we can start with to identify how we are feeling. Then, as we move outward, the emotions will become more detailed and nuanced, allowing us to get into the details of our feelings.

Take a moment and familiarize yourself with the feeling wheel so that during times of great emotional intensity, you can take a moment and explore what it is that you're feeling. It can also be helpful to take a minute, several times during the day, and ask, what am I feeling?

Knowing our emotional weather can create much insight into how we respond to the world.

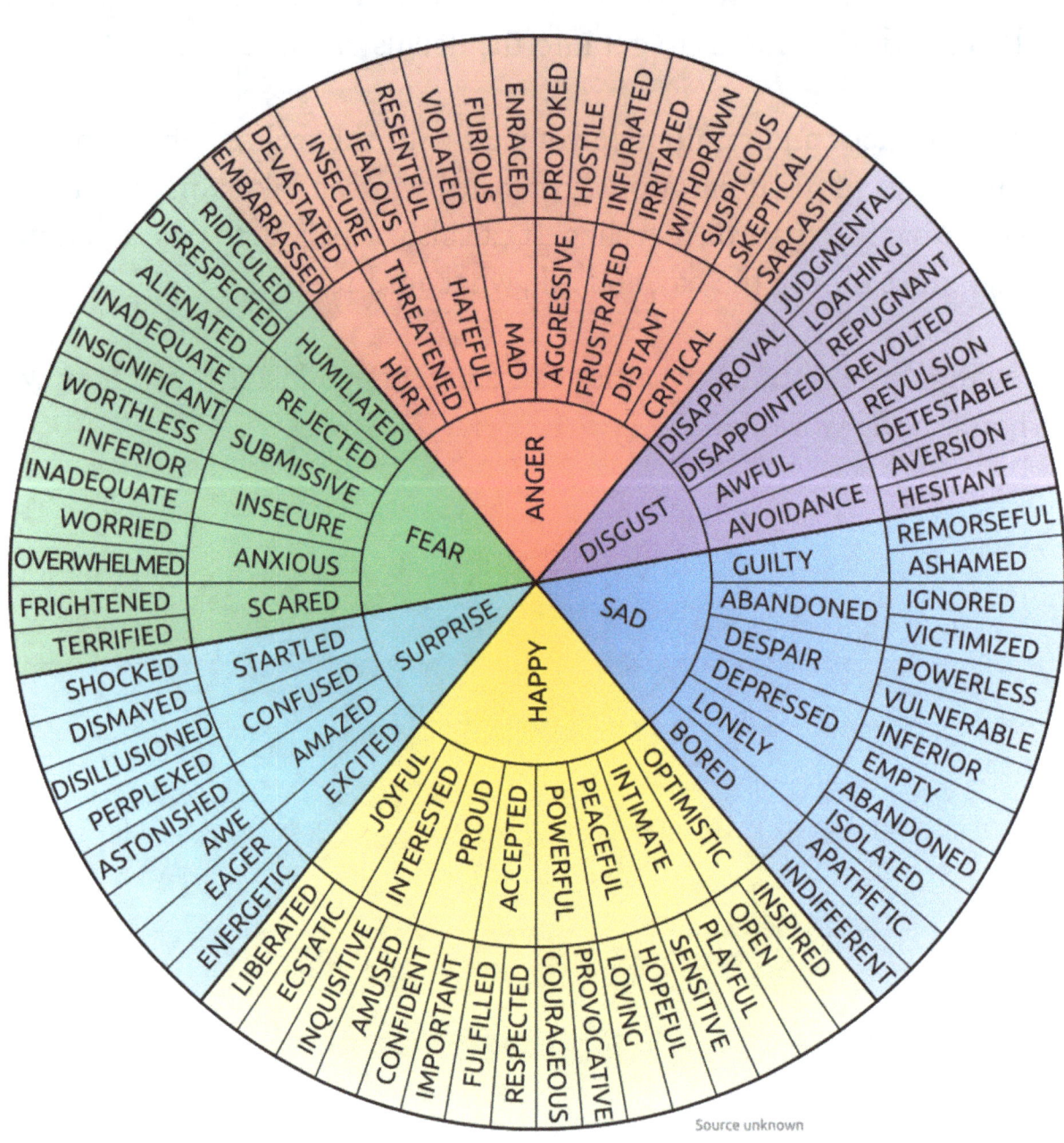

Source unknown

So, what are you feeling at this moment? Take a moment and explore what emotions are present for you.

Please know that we can have multiple emotions at the same time. We can have seemingly contradictory emotions at the same time. For example, we can simultaneously hold anger, love, sadness, and happiness.

Our emotions can be a lot like weather and change rapidly. They can feel like storms, or they can feel like a sunny day. Sometimes, we have rain and a rainbow at the same time. However, just like the weather, emotions are impermanent and will pass.

So, one part of having self-compassion is recognizing that we have complex emotions and that this is normal and okay.

Identifying and navigating our internal emotional weather becomes an essential tool in recovery.

Compassionate Reflection

What is your emotional weather today? What emotions are present for you in this moment?

Ex. I'm feeling proud of myself with some anxiety and depression.

_____

_____

_____

_____

What emotions do you try to feel most of the time?

Ex. I'm always trying to pretend I'm happy even when I'm not; I'm always trying to be tough and not show fear or sadness.

_____

_____

_____

_____

What emotions do you try NOT to feel?

Ex. Sadness, fear, shame, guilt, embarrassment

_____

_____

_____

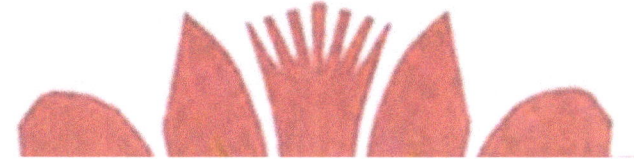

Were any emotions not allowed in your house growing up?

Ex. Sadness: I was always told to man up and that boys don't cry. So, I tried to hide my sadness. No one ever really talked about their vulnerable emotions in my house growing up.

_____
_____
_____
_____

What emotions most often caused you to use substances?

Ex. My anxiety always cause me to pick up. Every time I had the slightest bit of anxiety, I drank, and it worked until it didn't. I always used coke when I was feeling sad to lift my mood.

_____
_____
_____
_____
_____
_____
_____
_____
_____

When you think about the most difficult emotion for you to sit with, think about what words of kindness may help you in this moment.

For example, if you're feeling sadness, think about what you would tell a friend going through the same emotion. What would you tell your child going through the exact same thing? And see if you can offer yourself some words of kindness, love, inspiration, encouragement, or just loving acceptance for what you're going through.

Compassionate Reflection

What emotion do you most struggle with allowing yourself to feel?

Ex. I have no idea what to do with my guilt; I struggle with letting people know I'm sad. I have no clue what to do when I'm feeling anxious or having a panic attack.

_____
_____
_____
_____
_____

What compassion can you offer yourself when you have this particular emotion?

Ex. It's normal to get sad sometimes; life can be challenging. Maybe I can try to cry and let it out, and maybe I can take a chance to let someone I trust know I'm having a hard day and let them be there for me a little; it may feel nice not to have to do this alone.

_____
_____
_____
_____
_____

THE VOLCANO

1. You must let the pain visit.
2. You must allow it to teach you.
3. You must not allow it to overstay.

Ijeoma Umebinyuo

For many people, we learn to suppress our emotions in childhood. Growing up, we learn that certain emotions are unacceptable in society or in our homes.

For example, some men are taught that sadness or fear is unacceptable for them to express. Some women are told to be quiet or make themselves small, so they learn to suppress powerful emotions.

For others, sadness or vulnerabilities were not expressed in their families of origin; only anger and frustration were.

Many people learn to suppress their genuine emotions as a skill to survive the environments they grew up in and around.

Pushing or suppressing emotions is much like creating a volcano. You put all your emotions deep below the surface and periodically, and eventually, they explode. They often explode in a very messy and painful way.

Or you can think of suppressing emotions as a dark closet in your brain that's become overfilled, and when you try to open the door, everything falls on top of you.

So, instead of stuffing our emotions and suppressing them, one of the skills we will work on is acknowledging each emotion as it presents itself.

Think of emotions like a moment of emotional weather. For example, let's say you're having sadness. I like to think of sadness like rainy weather. We have a couple of options when we feel sad (it's raining).

One option is to walk outside in the rain and tell ourselves it's not raining! You say to yourself, I'm fine, but still, you're getting drenched with rain; it doesn't help you, right?

Another option is to say that it shouldn't be raining. It's unfair that it's raining. I don't want there to be rain, yet it's still raining, and you're still sad. Now you're getting wet, AND you're upset that it's raining in the first place.

The third option is to acknowledge and meet ourselves with compassion to offer ourselves what we need in this moment. Yes, it's raining, and I need an umbrella because that will make it a little bit easier for me to get through the storm. I may even need a friend to drive me where I'm going instead of walking because the storm is so difficult.

Our emotions are the same. We can either push them away. We can talk to the universe and say how unfair it is that we're feeling what we're experiencing, or we can accept and acknowledge that this is a moment of emotional weather and try to meet ourselves with compassion and offer ourselves the tools we need to navigate the moment as best we can.

Tell yourself that you can meet any emotion with compassion and loving action. Say to yourself- I can use my tools to navigate this moment compassionately, and this emotion is temporary; it has a beginning, a middle, and an end.

Compassionate Reflection

What emotions do you suppress or avoid the most?

Ex. I stuff down my shame; I have pushed my childhood abuse down so far that I can't even remember all of it. I have trouble standing up for myself because I feel guilty, so I let people walk all over me and suppress my anger.

_____

_____

_____

_____

_____

_____

_____

How do they explode or erupt if I hold emotions in or suppress them too long?

Ex. I explode on people, and they have no idea where it's coming from; I isolate and ignore everyone in my life.

_____

_____

_____

_____

_____

_____

What kindness do you need most when you are feeling these emotions? What would you tell a friend going through the exact same thing?

Ex. It can be hard to feel what I'm feeling; but it's safe to let it wash over me. It's going to be okay, and this feeling is not going to last forever; I don't have to do this alone, I can reach out for support. Remember, I'm worth taking care of and loving through hard times. I don't have to make things worse by using. I'm so loveable and worth taking care of.

RIDING THE WAVE

"You can't stop the waves, but you can learn to surf."

Jon Kabat-Zinn

We can learn to ride the wave of emotion. We can learn to ride the wave of a craving. In addiction, riding the wave of craving is called urge surfing. Alan Martlett, the founder of Mindfulness-Based Relapse Prevention, created the term urge surfing.

Emotions and cravings are very similar in that they both cause waves. We can learn to surf these waves anytime we're having a moment of difficulty with our present-moment experiences.

With all waves, there's a beginning where it starts, and you're triggered; there's a middle where it builds in intensity, and it reaches the crescendo, which is where most people decide to use a substance or to explode emotionally. Then there's the de-escalation, the calm down period, where you're high, and the emotion is temporarily gone, or you've exploded on someone and are dealing with the aftermath.

The skill that I would like to work on for this time of emotional intensity or craving is learning to ride this wave without using and without exploding and learning to meet our experiences, whether a craving or an emotional moment, with kindness, acceptance, and grace.

So, how do we ride this wave? It takes deliberate and compassionate exploration of the moment. Here are a few steps you can take.

1. First, we name the emotion. (Remember, name it to tame it!)

   Ex. I'm feeling anxious and overwhelmed.

2. We ask ourselves where do I feel this emotion in my body?

   Ex. I feel like I can't breathe, and there is a lump in my throat.

3. What urges are coming up for me to manage or cope with this emotion?

   Ex. I want to drink and numb out.

4. Does this emotion remind me of any times in the past?

   Ex. These emotions remind me of my last break-up.

5. Is this an emotional trigger for me?

   Ex. Is this an emotion uncomfortable for me to sit with? Do I usually push this emotion away? Is this emotion painful for me?

6. What would soothe or calm me while experiencing this difficult emotion?

   Ex. I need a hug, talk to a friend, hear it will be okay, and take a hot bath.

7. Can I tell myself any words of compassion that will support me as I navigate this complex emotion? What would you say to a friend or a child going through the same thing, then offer those same words to yourself?

   Ex. I'm sorry you're having such a hard time. You're so loveable, and I'm here for you. This will pass, but I'm here for you while you're in the thick of it.

We have to feel it to heal it.

Compassionate Reflection

Think about a recent difficult emotion you had. Let's investigate it with compassion.

What caused it? What did it feel like in your body? Did it remind you of any other time in your life? Can you offer yourself some kindness as to how complex this emotion is for you to experience?

Ex. When I feel sad, I feel a lump in my throat. I start to beat myself up that I'm a crybaby. Then I get kind of mad at myself. It reminds me of how my ex always told me I overreact. Maybe I can let myself know it's okay and normal to feel sad sometimes; everyone does, and I can offer myself some care right now. I can lay outside and watch the sky, call my good friend, and remind myself it's safe to feel. Not everyone thinks of me like my ex did.

_____

_____

_____

_____

_____

_____

_____

_____

_____

_____

_____

THE HAND YOU ARE DEALT

"God, grant me the serenity to accept the things
I cannot change, the courage to change the things
I can, and the wisdom to know the difference."

The Serenity Prayer

One part of pushing away our emotions or experiences is not accepting or acknowledging they are there. We often do this because our emotions and our experiences are too painful or we are unsure of how we can navigate them, especially sober.

I'd like you to take a moment to explore what things in your life you have the most difficulty accepting.

I like to use the metaphor of the hand you are dealt. What have you been dealt in this lifetime that feels unfair? That has caused you suffering. What has been difficult for you to manage or accept?

I ask this so we can start acknowledging where the healing needs to take place and where the acceptance needs to occur.

Acceptance does not mean that what happened to me is okay. Acceptance does not mean that what happened to me wasn't unfair or abusive, or horrific.

What it does mean is that it did happen. It does mean that it did affect me. It does mean that I need healing in this area, and it does mean for me to start to heal, I have to acknowledge that the problem exists or that the pain exists.

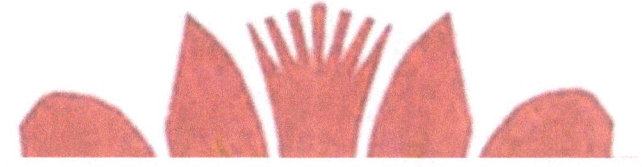

Compassionate Reflection

What hand are you holding? What cards are you holding? What in your life do you have the most difficulty accepting?

Ex. My hand is I'm an addict, I have childhood abuse, I was robbed and have PTSD, and I'm single and lonely. I have the most trouble accepting that I'm actually addicted.

_____

_____

_____

_____

_____

_____

What emotions come up when you look at your hand?

Ex. I feel like it's not fair I've had so much trauma, and that makes me feel sad; I even get mad at God when I look at all of this. I get overwhelmed and want to stop reading this workbook.

_____

_____

_____

_____

_____

_____

What kindness can you offer to the child who suffered?

Ex. She did nothing wrong; she had no idea what an abuser was or that it could be a family member she trusted. She was just a child being loving and naïve. She was worthy of being cared for and cared for, not abused.

_____

_____

_____

_____

_____

What kindness can you offer to how hard it has been to be stuck in addiction?

Ex. Nobody understands how often I've tried to quit or how lousy this makes me feel; they only see that I keep using. I want to stop using and know I'm worth taking care of myself. I have strength and know I don't have to do this all alone.

_____

_____

_____

_____

_____

_____

What kindness can you offer to yourself because you have had so much trauma?

Ex. Trauma is no joke. It's changed the way I see myself and made me scared of things I used to think were no big deal. I now realize that trauma has changed my brain, too, and I might need therapy to learn how to heal from this. It's not my fault that my trauma happened, but getting help is my responsibility.

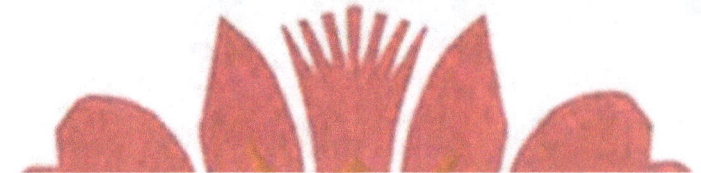

What compassion can you offer yourself that your mental health has been challenging for you to manage?

Ex. For so many years, I didn't even know that I had depression and anxiety. I just knew that I'd rather stay to myself inside of the house. It's been so hard for me to open up about being sad all of the time and having trouble talking to people I don't know. I can start to make changes in baby steps. But I didn't know about mental health or the help that was out there until I started talking about it.

_____

_____

_____

_____

_____

_____

_____

_____

_____

_____

_____

_____

_____

_____

_____

_____

_____

THE PAUSE

"A pause is a suspension of activity, a time of temporary disengagement when we are no longer moving toward any goal. . .. The pause can occur in the midst of almost any activity and can last for an instant, for hours or for seasons of our life…"

Tara Brach

Right now, some of you may have complicated or painful emotions. When experiencing a crisis or intense emotions, we often want to move fast to have it go away as soon as possible.

However, as we have learned, sometimes there is no immediate resolution, and sometimes we have to sit with discomfort.

The next skill, "the pause," can be helpful when you feel stuck in discomfort or think you need an immediate resolution; the pause can help to slow us down.

Sometimes, the best thing we can do is <u>nothing</u>.

Sometimes, the best thing we can do is take a moment, explore what is going on with us, and breathe. If you need to breathe for the next hour, it's okay to sit with your experience with compassion.

It's okay to feel what you're feeling; allow yourself to feel what you're feeling and breathe through it. If you need to, you can call someone and talk about what's happening with you. You can journal what emotions are coming up. You can hug your dog or cat or look at nature, sit outside, and watch the clouds go by.

The skill that we can learn in this moment of emotional difficulty is to pause. The world that we live in often wants us to move really fast. Our technology, the TV, the traffic, our jobs. It all moves very quickly, but that is not the speed of nature, so try to take a moment to pause and ask yourself:

What am I feeling? What am I thinking? What is showing up in my body? Does this remind me of any other time in my life? What kindness do I need at this moment?

And if all this feels like too much, it's okay to lie on the floor and breathe for a few moments and just be.

We can always move from DOING to BEING.

I read somewhere that giant trees have seasons of growth and seasons of rest. I like to think about how, throughout nature, there are seasons of growth and seasons of rest.

There will be some days when you're very productive and others when it takes all you can to wake up and wash your face. And both of these are okay. With both of these, we can have compassion for what we are going through.

We will have seasons where we are our "best self," our most productive or happy self, seasons where we just maintain, seasons where we have great difficulty, and seasons of loss or illness, and all of these are to be expected.

Remember, even fancy sports cars can't run 100 mph forever. They need an oil change, time to cool the engine, etc. Everything needs to pause to be refueled and taken care of, and you are no different.

You can pause for five minutes and allow yourself to breathe. You can type in healing frequencies, meditation music, or white/brown noise online if silence is difficult. These are different sounds that aid in relaxation.

So spend the next 5 to 10 minutes just stretching the body, sitting still, or lying down, and allow yourself to breathe and explore what is going on for you in this moment. Explore using the pause.

Compassionate Reflection

What permission can you give yourself to pause and reflect?

Ex. It's safe for me to slow down. I don't always have to be going 1000 miles per hour. I can take a beat, let myself breathe, and even remind myself it will be okay.

_____

_____

_____

_____

_____

_____

_____

_____

_____

_____

_____

_____

_____

_____

_____

_____

_____

_____

THE SPEED OF NATURE

"Slowing down is medicine."

Unknown

When life feels too fast or overwhelming, it's often an indicator that it's time to slow down. Nature has a unique way of assisting us in slowing down. If you ever find your mind racing or feel like everything is too intense, I'd encourage you to look at the sky or watch the clouds. Look at the treetops and watch them slowly move in the wind. Or even look to the ground and find a tiny insect making its way across the soil. Maybe you could watch a river moving slowly, watch the waves of the ocean crashing in rhythm, or maybe it's a bird in the sky that you gently watch fly to the right and left.

Nature can be a unique tool to use with our pause skill and another tool we can put in the toolbox. We do not need to move the speed of the Internet; we do not need to move the speed of traffic; we do not need to move the speed of capitalism; we do not even need to move the speed of our racing thoughts.

Sometimes, the best thing we can do is to slow down and offer ourselves an opportunity to recharge.

Remember, you ARE nature 😊

Compassionate Reflection

What in nature gives you the most peace? Where can you go in nature to experience slowing down?

Ex. The ocean, the forest, and watching the clouds. I can go in my backyard and watch the birds and also watch the treetops sway in the wind.

_____

_____

_____

_____

_____

_____

How do you feel when you are slowing down?

Ex. I feel stir-crazy! I feel like I should be doing something. I feel peaceful

_____

_____

_____

_____

_____

_____

_____

THE GRIEF

"Everything I've ever let go of has claw marks on it."

David Foster Wallace

Just because you know that you must quit using substances, does it mean that you're not going to miss it. Just because you have to let go of people that you know are toxic or unsafe for your recovery doesn't mean that you're not going to miss them. Knowing you can't go to the sports bar anymore doesn't mean you won't miss that community on game day.

Something that people don't talk enough about in recovery is the grief that comes when you let go of using.

For a lot of people, drugs, and alcohol have been the longest and most consistent relationship in your life.

Substances may have been the most consistent means of comfort, the longest relationship, and the steadiest source of ease when life got hard. It's okay to honor that and to grieve it.

Letting go of your use can bring up a lot of feelings of grief, longing, sadness, or even fear. This doesn't mean that your use is good for you, but it does mean that grief might be a phase in your recovery.

It's okay to miss the benefits you felt from using. You used it for a long time because it felt good. You used it for a long time because it helped you manage emotions, feel something when you felt numb, feel connected, get through the day, sleep, manage your anxiety, etc.

It's okay to miss the good that it gave you. It can be a helpful question to ask yourself: how did my substance use help me? Because then, once you have an answer, you can identify a sober coping skill that meets that same need.

It's okay to grieve what you miss about it. For a lot of you, you may have started using when you were very young, when you were a teenager, or, for some, even younger. So, your drugs and alcohol may have been a tool that you've used to manage your life experiences for *many* years. Now, you may not know how to manage your experiences without it. It's okay to grieve that. Grieving that you no longer have this tool you used for many years is okay.

This doesn't mean that you should continue to use; it simply means that it's normal to feel sadness, it's normal to feel confusion, and it's normal to feel grief as you start to walk away from your addiction. (You're so brave for doing this).

Compassionate Reflection

What were the things I enjoyed most about my substance use?

Ex. I had a lot of fun; I used to laugh all the time, was much braver and adventurous, and felt like I could talk to anybody; it helped me sleep and reduced my anxiety.

_____

_____

_____

_____

_____

_____

_____

Can I find the same relief in any other way?

Ex. I can learn about sleep hygiene, I can get on medication for my anxiety, I can go to therapy, I can start meditating, and I can remind myself that growth and healing take time; I can start new hobbies to have more fun.

_____

_____

_____

_____

_____

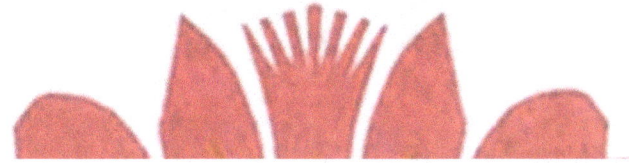

What am I afraid to let go of?

Ex. I'm afraid to let go of my street life; I'm so scared to let go of the personality I had when I was high; I'm scared to let go of my old friends; I'm afraid that I'll never relax again, I'm scared I'll feel out of control sober.

_____
_____
_____
_____
_____
_____
_____
_____

What am I going to miss the most?

Ex. I will miss feeling so relaxed and uninhibited; I will miss being able to zone out and forget my stress.

_____
_____
_____
_____
_____
_____
_____
_____

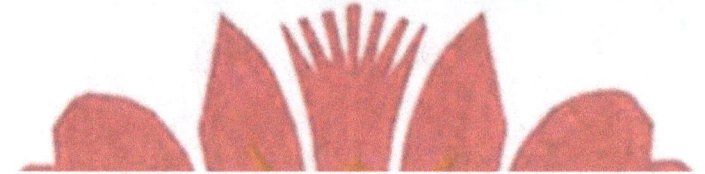

What feelings come up for me when I think about letting go of my substance use? Remember, we can hold many emotions at once!

Ex. I get sad, scared, worried, excited, hopeful, proud.

_____

_____

_____

_____

_____

_____

_____

What compassion can you give to yourself that this letting go is hard for you?

Ex. It's okay to grieve, letting go of the familiar; it's all I've known in my adult life. New things can be terrifying for everyone. I can offer kindness or support when it feels too much.

_____

_____

_____

_____

_____

_____

_____

YOUR LOVE BUCKET

"One of the best guides to how to be self-loving is to give ourselves the love we are often dreaming about receiving from others."

Bell Hooks

Often, when someone is engaged in a full-time addiction, their own needs, whether physical, mental, or spiritual, can get neglected.

Just because you put down the substance doesn't mean you automatically become equipped with the necessary tools to fulfill your needs.

I like to think of our needs as a love bucket. We often try to pour into others from an empty bucket, making us feel depleted and empty.

An essential recovery tool is learning how to fill our love bucket emotionally, physically, mentally, and spiritually.

So, take a moment to reflect on what makes you feel nourished, full, and abundant emotionally. What makes you feel nourished and abundant mentally? What is it that makes you feel nourished and abundant physically? What is it that makes you feel nourished and abundant spiritually?

Spending time daily feeding into your needs and seeing what it feels like to learn to take care of yourself wholly can be a helpful recovery tool.

In the long run, you will be much better able to fill or pour into others when you are nourished and pouring into yourself. Self-care can be challenging, but it's important to do it anyway. You can start with the basics.

Let's go over some examples.

To nourish yourself physically, eat three meals a day, drink water, get enough rest, take vitamins and needed medications, move your body regularly, and spend time outdoors.

To nourish yourself mentally: Read/write, listen to podcasts, meditate, journal, go back to school, watch "good news" (look up good news networks online) and have a clean and safe environment.

To nourish yourself spiritually: Spend time in nature, meditate, attend religious services, repeat mantras, practice yoga, pray, and speak with spiritual teachers and advisors.

To nourish yourself emotionally: Identify your emotions, create a safe space to feel, offer yourself compassion when experiencing difficult emotions, and find safe people to talk with.

Compassionate Reflection

How can I feed my love bucket emotionally, physically, and spiritually?

Ex. Emotionally, I can start going to therapy and journaling; physically, I want to start walking my dog more and jumping rope; spiritually, I want to get back into meditation and yoga.

_____

_____

_____

_____

_____

_____

Do I tend to feed more into others? How does this leave me feeling?

Ex. When I'm tired and have had a hard day, and I do for others instead of caring for myself, I get even more exhausted, and I also feel resentful sometimes that they don't look out for me like I look out for them. It makes me think some of my relationships might not be reciprocated.

_____

_____

_____

_____

_____

THE MYTH OF PERFECTION

"Mistakes are a fact of life.
It is the response to error that counts."

Nikki Giovanni

Question:

Name one thing in your life you've learned without making a mistake.

I'll wait... 😊

The answer is there is *nothing*!

When you learn to walk, you fall flat on your face. When you learn to talk, you say goo goo and ga ga, and it doesn't make any sense. You make a mistake when you learn any skill, whether writing or riding a bike. At your first job, you made plenty of mistakes.

Making mistakes is the ONLY way we learn!

However, we tend to beat ourselves up whenever we make a mistake. We tend to be very harsh to ourselves anytime we make a mistake as if the harshness would somehow prevent future mistakes.

The thing is, the *harshness doesn't prevent future mistakes*. It just creates more shame when those mistakes come up. It creates more self-criticism when those mistakes come up. It makes us believe that our mistakes somehow reflect our worth, intelligence, or abilities.

Since we now understand that mistakes are the only way to learn, what if we apply compassion when we make mistakes? What if when we make a mistake, we take a moment and reflect on what it is we are learning from the mistake? What is the lesson? What is the takeaway? What is the insight?

Can I offer myself kindness that making mistakes is a hard way to learn?

If we take a moment to ask ourselves these questions, we will learn from our experiences and continue to evolve and grow. This is where we get true power: when we develop the insight to learn from our experiences versus if we continue to shame ourselves and beat ourselves up every time we make a mistake.

Eventually, if we blame ourselves for our mistakes, we stop trying and stepping outside our comfort zone. We eventually stop trying to grow, and our life becomes smaller and smaller. It becomes a predictable life, *which may have fewer mistakes, but it also has less wonder and growth.*

Our opportunity is to start becoming friends with our mistakes and learn how to grow from them and through them. We can befriend the process of making mistakes and learning from them. This becomes a powerful tool in our path of recovery. We are all messy, we are all imperfect, we are all a work in progress, and we are all doing the best we can, one day at a time.

Allow your mistakes to be your teachers, but do not allow them to define you.

Compassionate Reflection

What mistakes have you made that can you meet with more compassion?

Ex. Getting addicted in the first place, staying addicted for so long, blacking out, and saying hurtful things.

_____

_____

_____

_____

What compassionate statements can you tell yourself about that mistake?

Ex. If I had known better, I would have done better, but I didn't know. I had no idea I was addicted; I just thought I didn't care about other people or myself. I realized I didn't know how to stop, so I blamed myself. I'm learning that addiction is a disease that requires treatment. I'm learning that I'm still worth loving and forgiving.

_____

_____

_____

_____

_____

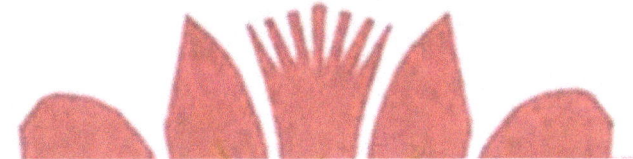

What did you learn from those mistakes? Can you change your behavior or insight as a result?

Ex. I'm learning that recovery is a process and addiction is a serious disease. I'm learning that I don't have to do this alone. I'm going to therapy, attending AA, and even biking again. I can learn from my mistakes, but they no longer have to define me.

MOTIVATION COMES AFTER ACTION

"If nothing changes, nothing changes."

Alcoholics Anonymous

A lot of people think because they've had so many negative experiences with addiction, that they would automatically be motivated to stop using or to change behavior.

Unfortunately, motivation does not always proceed action.

Often, what we're motivated to do is what we've done the most in our lives or what behaviors are connected to the strongest chemicals in our brains.

If you spent the last 20 or 30 years getting high, the last thing you're going to be motivated to do is to be sober. This doesn't mean that you don't *want* to be sober; you probably do, or you wouldn't be reading this workbook, but your motivation is likely still to use substances, and your motivation is likely not to want to sit with your difficult emotions or experiences. *I say all of this to say- it's okay if you're not motivated to do anything healthy or sober.*

The skill we're learning is not being motivated and doing it *anyway*.

I want you to think about if you've ever been out of shape and you thought about going to the gym. You probably did not want to go to the gym but knew you needed to. And the first few weeks you went, you were out of breath, maybe you threw up, and it was a challenging experience.

However, you start to notice that after a few weeks, you begin to feel better after you work out, even though you don't always want to show up, and you start to feel the benefits of working out or eating better. It's only weeks after you start this behavior, and sometimes months, that you have an internal motivation to go to the gym or eat your vegetables.

Your recovery will often feel the same. You won't want to go to a meeting, you won't want to stay sober, you won't want to investigate your emotions. You won't want to go to bed early or take vitamins and medications. You won't want to stay home instead of going out to the bar, and it's okay to honor all of this. You won't want to go to therapy or talk about what you've kept inside for so many years.

Explore having some compassion that it's hard to take better care of yourself when you don't have the motivation.

But I still want you to make the effort to change your behaviors for the better! *Just don't beat yourself up if you're not motivated.* If you're not motivated to do it, recognize that that's common and that motivation will come months and, sometimes, years later.

Remember, your brain is still healing! So right now, the world will feel raw and uncomfortable, but I want you to take care of yourself anyway. You are worth it!

Compassionate Reflection

Can you think of a time you changed a behavior? Was it hard to get motivated initially?

Ex. Quitting smoking: I didn't want to stop, and the first few weeks were horrible! But over time, I craved it less and less and started to feel better!

_____

_____

_____

_____

_____

_____

How were you able to encourage yourself despite not being motivated?

Ex. It's normal not to want to stop using or to go to recovery meetings; let me take it one baby step at a time. I'll look up the NA meetings one day. Find the directions the next day and show up on the third day. I've got this!

_____

_____

_____

_____

_____

How can you encourage yourself now?

Ex. Look at me reading this workbook! Look at me staying sober in this moment. I am learning how to care for myself! I can do hard things!

_____

_____

_____

_____

_____

_____

_____

What are you willing to start doing, even though you don't want to?

Ex. Go to AA, exercise more, call my old friends, and eat vegetables!

_____

_____

_____

_____

_____

_____

_____

_____

_____

_____

Early recovery is crucial for establishing positive habits and building a foundation for your best sober and fulfilling life. Here are 50 positive activities to consider during the early stages of recovery:

1. Attend support group meetings (e.g., AA, NA).
2. Work with a sponsor.
3. Start a gratitude journal.
4. Create a relapse prevention plan.
5. Attend outpatient treatment or therapy sessions.
6. Establish a daily routine.
7. Explore mindfulness and meditation.
8. Practice deep-breathing exercises.
9. Exercise regularly.
10. Take up jogging or walking.
11. Join a fitness class.
12. Engage in yoga or tai chi.
13. Volunteer for a local charity.
14. Attend a recovery-focused workshop or seminar.
15. Connect with sober friends.
16. Reconnect with family members.
17. Set short-term and long-term goals.
18. Learn a new skill or hobby.
19. Take a cooking or art class.
20. Attend relapse prevention groups.
21. Establish a healthy sleep routine.
22. Explore hobbies that promote relaxation.
23. Attend recreational activities in a sober environment.
24. Create a sober support network.
25. Develop a healthy nutrition plan.
26. Practice self-compassion and self-care.
27. Attend a recovery-related event.
28. Join a sober sports league.

29. Take up gardening.
30. Attend a church or spiritual group.
31. Create a sober daily affirmation practice.
32. Start a book club with sober friends.
33. Take part in outdoor activities (e.g., hiking, biking).
34. Attend a recovery-themed art class.
35. Work on mending relationships.
36. Establish a routine for regular check-ins with a counselor.
37. Plan and participate in weekend activities.
38. Explore educational opportunities.
39. Engage in stress-reducing activities (e.g., meditation, massage).
40. Attend holistic wellness workshops.
41. Practice mindfulness-based stress reduction (MBSR).
42. Take up a musical instrument.
43. Participate in a recovery-focused retreat.
44. Attend community support events.
45. Develop a sober social calendar.
46. Explore local museums or art galleries.
47. Practice positive visualization.
48. Attend a comedy show or improv night.
49. Connect with a sober mentor.
50. Explore nature through hiking or camping trips.

Engage in activities that inspire you, bring you joy or spark your interests. Early recovery is a time of self-discovery, and finding activities that bring joy and fulfillment and support your sobriety is crucial. Consider working closely with a treatment team, therapist, or support group to identify the activities that align with your goals and values.

Can you create a weekly schedule to keep yourself accountable?

Try to identify positive activities to incorporate into each day.

WEEK
at a glance

Mon	
Tue	
Wed	
Thurs	
Fri	
Sat	
Sun	

BE YOUR OWN CHEERLEADER (BYOC)

"Let today be the day you are kind to yourself and focus on believing what is beautiful and true. And this does not mean you ignore your imperfections. It means, in spite of them, you believe there is beauty to you."

Morgan Harper Nichols

There will not be a crowd roaring with applause when you don't light that cigarette. No one will stop and give you a high five when you drive past the liquor store, and don't stop. No one is going to clap and scream for you when you don't pick up the call from your drug dealer, who is just checking in to "make sure you're okay." This doesn't mean that you can't be your own cheerleader.

The skill I'd like to focus on is learning to celebrate all your successes, big or small. Every time you want to use substances and you don't, celebrate! Every time you take care of yourself in a different way, celebrate! Every time you want to get high and don't, celebrate! Every time you catch your thinking and recognize that it's harsh, and you change it to compassionate self-talk, celebrate! Every time you take your vitamins, eat healthily, or move your body instead of binge-eating or watching television, celebrate!

We tend to make our criticism louder than our celebration.

Learn to become your own inner cheerleader. Throughout the day, take a moment and offer yourself a tiny moment of "woo-hoo"! A tiny moment of- "You did this!" or "You've got this!" or "Look at you, kid, you're making a change!" or "Brush your shoulders off!" Give yourself that praise.

No one else will necessarily do this work for you, but it doesn't mean that it's not important work.

In recovery, if we don't celebrate our successes, who will? Sure, you get a chip at meetings, and you have your family or friends who support you, which feels great. We need daily, hourly, or minute-by-minute encouragement, support, and celebration for all the mini-victories occurring on any given day.

Your addiction doesn't take a day off, so neither should your cheerleader!

Compassionate Reflection

What praise can you offer yourself over your behavior change in the last six months?

Ex. It's pretty awesome that I stopped hanging out with people who get high as much; I started therapy, which was scary for me, so that took bravery, and I go walking outside more, which is hard for me to get motivated, so good for me!

_____
_____
_____
_____
_____

The last month?

Ex. I need to give myself some kudos that I stopped drinking this month! It took so much bravery from me, and I'm still terrified, to be honest. I need to remember how much self-love it takes to try something like sobriety.

_____
_____
_____
_____
_____

The last week?

Ex. I had a tough day last week at work, and all I wanted to do was get high. I'm super proud of myself that not only did I not get high or be rude to anyone, but I also walked away and just did some deep breathing. I can make changes, which gives me hope for the future!

_____
_____
_____
_____
_____
_____
_____

The last hour?

Ex. I'm learning I don't have to respond to everything immediately. I can sit with things and make a decision later. It takes a lot of patience, which is hard for me. I'm grateful that I'm practicing patience and starting to believe I can make changes slowly!

_____
_____
_____
_____
_____

How can you reward yourself with a safe treat?

Ex. Buy myself a nice meal, a new haircut or speak to myself more kindly.

YOU ARE A PICKLE:

The Science of Addiction

"Neuroscience is a baby science, a mere century old, and our scientific understanding of the brain is nowhere near where we'd like it to be. We know more about the moons of Jupiter than what is inside of our skulls."

Matt Haig

So, let's get into some of the science behind addiction. Understanding science can be a helpful tool in reducing shame.

Many people rely on willpower to stop using and then get upset with themselves or hate themselves when their willpower is not enough. *Willpower will never be enough* on its own.

The reason is that:

Addiction is a disease.

Addiction rewires the brain.

Our brains are constantly responding to their environments, and as a result, the brain can "rewire" and "re-organize" and structurally and functionally change itself based on its experiences. This is called neuroplasticity. This means that our brains are constantly making connections based on our behaviors and the associated chemicals that go along with our behaviors.

Addiction has re-wired the part of the brain that is connected to *survival*-based activities. Addiction is now on the same highway as eating, intimacy, and shelter, which are required for the species' survival.

What happens in the brain when we engage in these survival-based activities is that our brain gives us dopamine as a reward so that we continue to do these activities (eating, sex, and shelter) so that the species survives.

However, because addiction gives us *much more* dopamine than these other survival-based activities and is now on the same highway, we will begin to choose addiction over what we need to survive.

So, what happens is our brain says to us we need our substance of choice, whether it be alcohol or cocaine, more than we need food, more than we need relationships, more than we need housing, *more than we need anything!*

The longer that you have fed this highway of addiction, the stronger it gets. So, this is why you crave something that destroys your life. This is why you would rather use substances than eat. This is why you would rather use substances than have relationships.

The brain has been rewired to say, not only do I want drugs and alcohol, I NEED drugs and alcohol for my very SURVIVAL!

This can be confusing when you know that drugs and alcohol are ruining your life, ruining your relationships, and creating a very uncomfortable existence.

People often ask, "Why do I crave something that ruins my life?". "There must be something wrong with me." There's nothing wrong with you.

Addiction is complicated. Addiction is influenced by a combination of genetic, biological, psychological, and environmental factors.

All of these factors, and more, contribute to the complexity of addiction.

Most importantly, you must remember that your brain has been structurally re-wired by the continued substance use.

And here's the thing…

Once these highways in the brain are created, *they cannot be destroyed.* They hang out forever, so this is why I called this chapter the pickle.

Once a cucumber becomes a pickle, it cannot return to being a cucumber. Once a grape becomes a raisin, it cannot return to being a grape. YOU ARE A PICKLE, and some grief may come along with knowing that your brain will always be an addicted brain.

We're going to get more into cravings in the next chapter, but first, there's a level of acceptance you must come to that your brain may crave for a very long time, something deadly that destroys your life.

You crave not because you are a bad person, not because you are weak, not because you don't have intelligence or willpower, but simply because the structure and chemistry in your brain have been changed **permanently**.

The good news is we can create NEW highways in the brain.

The old highways don't disappear; however, we can give them some competition.

We can create new highways that connect to chemicals of pleasure and happiness, such as dopamine, serotonin, and oxytocin. By engaging in pleasurable activities and hobbies and spending time with people who care about us and bring us joy, we can create new highways in the brain that bring us pleasure.

Remember, your old highways are much stronger, so they will be your default for quite a long time.

That doesn't mean that you shouldn't build the new highways. Remember that you may be motivated to ride the old highways much more strongly than you will be motivated to ride the new ones.

Build anyway.

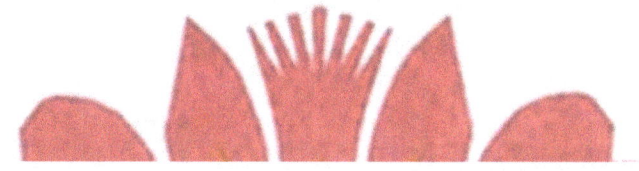

Compassionate Reflection

What comes up when you learn your brain has been rewired to crave substances?

Ex. It makes me feel less crazy cause it's my actual brain that has been changed; it's not just me wanting to self-destruct. I realize now it's going to be difficult to stop using because of the cravings I will have, but it's not impossible.

_____

_____

_____

_____

What forgiveness can you offer yourself for not knowing that a lot of your behaviors were driven by a survival-based craving for dopamine and not a sign of weakness?

Ex. These last few years have been hard, and I have always wondered why I'm doing something that is killing me. Now I know, and I feel lighter with less self-hate inside.

_____

_____

_____

_____

_____

What positive activities can you start in your life to give your addiction some competition?

Ex. Art, exercise, boating, fishing, walking in nature, crafting, music, travel, spirituality.

_____

_____

_____

_____

_____

_____

_____

_____

_____

_____

_____

_____

_____

_____

_____

_____

_____

_____

_____

_____

THE ADDICTION MONSTER IS HUNGRY

One evening, an elderly Cherokee told his grandson
about a battle that goes on inside each of us.

He said, "My son, the battle is between two 'wolves' inside us all. One
is evil. It is anger, envy, jealousy, sorrow, regret, greed, arrogance, self-
pity, guilt, resentment, inferiority, lies, false pride, superiority, and ego.

The other is good. It is joy, peace, love, hope, serenity, humility, kindness,
benevolence, empathy, generosity, truth, compassion, and faith."

"The same fight is going on inside you—and
inside every other person, too."

The grandson thought about it for a minute and then
asked his grandfather, "Which wolf wins?"

The old Cherokee simply replied,

"The one that you feed."

So now that you have an understanding that your brain requires dopamine for survival and will go to the source where the dopamine is the strongest, understand that, as you stop substance, you're going to crave substance because it gives you more dopamine than other survival-based activities and has created itself a very strong highway in the brain.

Coming to terms with the fact that you're going to crave something that is destroying your life is a necessary part of recovery.

So many people experience shame for cravings or try to deny they are craving. Neither response is helpful; shame and avoidance make us push away the cravings, and we never learn how to manage them.

We want to learn how you experience cravings because cravings will be different for each person. A lot of people try to ignore cravings. I always say ignoring cravings is like ignoring cockroaches. Do they go away if you ignore them? No way! They multiply. Cravings are the same!

So, let's take some time and explore how cravings start, how we experience them, and what to do about them.

What is needed to start a craving is a trigger. Triggers are often people, places, and things that your brain has associated with your addiction. In terms of people, this could be people that you used to use with, your dealer, your family, and other people that you see using in the street or at the bar.

Places that are triggers would be places that you historically would use; this could be the bar, the trap, your own living room, a bathroom or your own La-Z-Boy chair. People will have different people, places, and things that trigger them.

Lastly, *things* can also trigger us, so take a moment and think about what time of day you usually use. That time of day can be a trigger. The sound of a lighter, a soda can opening, seeing a sandwich baggie, lighting a cigarette, the smell of substance, the smell of cut grass or barbecue, or a football game can be a trigger. All these things can also be a trigger. Learning what triggers your addiction is very important.

You can avoid some triggers, but not all. So, learning to manage and better understand your triggers keeps you more prepared for the future. Once your brain gets triggered, your brain gives you a little bit of dopamine; it *primes you*. So, think about how you prime a lawnmower; you give it a little bit of gas to get the lawnmower started. Well, our brains are very much the same. Once there's a trigger that's associated with your substance use. The brain gives you a little bit of dopamine and says, go get more! Once your brain is primed, you are likely to crave your substance.

Learning to recognize and manage cravings is an essential tool for recovery.

Compassionate Reflection

What are your triggers to use?

Ex. Football, getting angry, anxiety, the smell of marijuana, payday, right after I get home from work is always a trigger.

_____
_____
_____
_____
_____
_____
_____
_____
_____
_____
_____
_____
_____
_____
_____
_____
_____
_____
_____
_____

After we have been primed with a little bit of dopamine, we start to crave. Cravings can occur physically, mentally, and emotionally. And again, each of us will experience cravings in our unique way.

Let's first talk about how the body experiences physical cravings. Think back to the last time you craved your substance and how it showed up in your body. You may feel all of sudden a tingly feeling, you may have what we call bubble guts or an excited stomach and have to use the bathroom right away, you may suddenly feel the need to pace around and feel unable to be still, your mouth might water, or you might have cottonmouth, or your head may feel dizzy.

Compassionate Reflection

How do your cravings show up for you physically?

Ex. My mouth waters, I get bubble guts and have to use the bathroom right away, I can't be still and have to pace, I feel kind of dizzy and lightheaded.

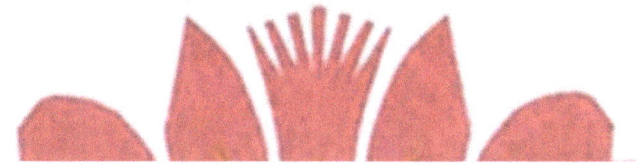

It can be helpful to separate you from your addiction. You are not your addiction. I want you to imagine that your addiction is a monster. Take a moment and envision the nastiest, ugliest monster that you've been feeding (very well) every day for 10, 20, 30, or 40 years.

Draw your addiction monster here:

Now, you've taken this monster, and you've put it in a cage and begun to starve it. First, what does it do? It rattles the bars! It gives you physical withdrawal symptoms. It makes you feel very uncomfortable, physically. But if that doesn't work, and you don't feed it after the withdrawal, what it will do is start to try and manipulate you *mentally*.

This can be confusing. Your addiction is going to try and manipulate you through your own thoughts.

Your addiction is going to use your own intelligence against you.

It becomes essential to understand how the addiction monster tries to manipulate your thoughts.

Remember YOU do not want to use substances, but your ADDICTION does!

You will experience cravings mentally. The best way to identify what thoughts are cravings is to take a moment and think about what you tell yourself *that you know is entirely untrue*. For example, the addiction monster will often try to manipulate the brain by telling us lies.

For example, "I can have only one," "I'm not addicted," "I am a social user," "It'll be different this time," "I've been sober for a month, and I can now go back to using socially." Or it will try and *negotiate*- "I can use marijuana instead of cocaine," "I can use beer instead of liquor," "I can use marijuana instead of alcohol."

Remember, the monster of addiction doesn't care what you feed it as long as it gets fed that good old dopamine. All these statements are intended to get you to pick up the substance and get the cycle started again.

One of the biggest thoughts that get people to pick up is F-it. Beware of the F-its!

Your addiction doesn't want you to care and wants you to give up.

Your addiction will also try and give you dangerous permission or appeal to your sense of independence, for example, saying, "I'm a grown man; no one can tell me what to do," or "I've worked a long day, and I deserve to relax."

The addiction monster will get you as *close* to the substance as possible. Addiction wants proximity to any substance. Addiction wants to get you as close to the substance as possible. It will tell you, "I'm going to the sports bar to see my friends," or "I'm going to the package store to buy a lotto ticket," all *LIES*! You are going to be in the same room as your substance.

Remember that addiction is trying to manipulate your thoughts to get you to pick up again. It can be helpful to write down your thoughts when you are craving and write your response to them or your comeback. Keep this with you on your phone or a piece of paper somewhere you can reference it regularly.

Do this preparation because when a craving shows up, and you've already been primed, you're going to be more likely to believe the lies that the addiction monster tells you. So, it's super helpful to have your comeback or your rethinking statements with you so that you can reference them and remind yourself that what the addiction monster is telling you is all lies.

Additionally, have the phone numbers of sober peers, sponsors, or substance use warmlines handy so that if your brain is highjacked, you can bring another brain into the discussion!

Compassionate Reflection

What lies does your addiction monster tell you?

Ex. I'm not that addicted; I can be a social user, I can have just one, that it's not that bad.

_____

_____

_____

_____

_____

_____

How does your addiction try to negotiate with you?

Ex. I know I can't have liquor, but I can have beer, I can't have coke, but I can have weed, I can't do brown liquor, but I can do clear, I'll have a few.

_____

_____

_____

_____

_____

_____

_____

What gives you the f-its? Or I'm a grown person, and nobody can tell me what to do thoughts?

Ex. Someone telling me I can't drink immediately makes me want to drink. When someone accuses me of using, I think I might as well because they already think I did. When my day is so awful, and I'm overwhelmed with life, I start to say f-it; it doesn't even matter if I'm sober today.

_____

_____

_____

_____

_____

_____

_____

_____

_____

_____

_____

_____

_____

_____

_____

_____

_____

We can also experience cravings emotionally. So, take a moment and think about the emotion you most often picked up over. Meaning, if every time you were sad, did you drink? If every time you were anxious, did you get high? If every time you're stressed out, did you use opiates?

The brain has made a connection between this emotion and the substance.

You may find that you crave when you have this particular emotion. Or even more confusingly, you may, for example, create the emotion. For instance, if every time you got angry, you drank, you might find yourself starting a fight over something dumb as an excuse to get angry enough to use to "calm down." If every time your PTSD was triggered and you used marijuana, you might find yourself watching the news or watching a war movie to activate your trauma symptoms as a reason to get high.

Much of this is subconscious, so be on the lookout for this.

This can be very confusing, so keep an eye on what emotions are attached to your use to become more aware that when you experience very normal emotions, you might also crave to use substances simultaneously.

Compassionate Reflection

What emotions did you most often use substances with?

Ex. ANGER, SADNESS, FEAR, GRIEF?

_____

_____

_____

_____

What triggers these emotions most often for you? (We may not be able to avoid the triggers, but we can become aware that they are emotional triggers)

Ex. Remembering my trauma, fights with family, being mistreated at work, feeling overwhelmed, being stressed about finances.

_____

_____

_____

_____

_____

_____

_____

So now that you recognize that you're craving, it's important to figure out what to do about it. Managing cravings can be broken down into three categories.

1. Express it
2. Soothe it
3. Distract it

First, we want to express to someone that we are craving. This is why it's essential to develop sober peers and recovery support through meetings, online support groups, spiritual communities, family members, hotlines, warm lines, hobby groups, or volunteering. No matter where you meet the sober peer, call someone and *tell on your disease*.

Your disease does not want you to tell on it. Addiction thrives in secrecy; addiction thrives in silence, and addiction thrives in isolation.

Your addiction wants you all to itself. So, the first part of managing a craving is to tell somebody what you're experiencing and get it off your chest. Talk about it! This will help you ride the wave of the craving and give you much-needed support.

Remember, if your brain has been highjacked, having another brain in the room can give you much-needed perspective.

Talking to someone about your craving helps you analyze and understand the trigger. You can discuss an action plan to manage this trigger the next time it appears with your peer. You can better learn to explore the trigger and how it shows up in your mind, body, and emotions.

For you future reference, here is a list of recovery hotlines and websites in the United States covering both mental health and substance abuse support:

Mental Health Hotlines:

1. **National Suicide Prevention Lifeline:**
   - Hotline: 1-800-273-TALK (1-800-273-8255)

2. **Crisis Text Line:**
   - Text "HELLO" to 741741

3. **SAMHSA National Helpline (Substance Abuse and Mental Health Services Administration):**
   - Helpline: 1-800-662-HELP (1-800-662-4357)

4. **Veterans Crisis Line:**
   - Hotline: 1-800-273-8255 (Press 1 for veterans) or dial 988

5. **The Trevor Project (LGBTQ+):**
   - Trevor Lifeline: 1-866-488-7386
   - Text "START" to 678678

6. **National Alliance on Mental Illness (NAMI) Helpline:**
   - Helpline: 1-800-950-NAMI (1-800-950-6264)

7. **Mental Health America:**
   - Website: www.mhanational.org

Substance Abuse and Addiction Recovery Hotlines:

1. SAMHSA National Helpline (Substance Abuse and Mental Health Services Administration):
- Helpline: 1-800-662-HELP (1-800-662-4357)

2. National Institute on Drug Abuse (NIDA) Helpline:
- Helpline: 1-800-662-4357

3. Alcoholics Anonymous (AA) Hotline:
- Hotline: 1-212-870-3400

4. Narcotics Anonymous (NA) Helpline:
- Helpline: 1-818-773-9999

5. SMART Recovery:
- Website: www.smartrecovery.org

6. Substance Abuse and Mental Health Services Administration (SAMHSA) Behavioral Health Treatment Services Locator:
- Website: www.findtreatment.samhsa.gov

General Support:

1. 211 (United Way):
- Dial 211 for information on local resources and services.

2. National Domestic Violence Hotline:
- Hotline: 1-800-799-SAFE (1-800-799-7233)

3. Rape, Abuse & Incest National Network (RAINN) National Sexual Assault Hotline:
- Hotline: 1-800-656-HOPE (1-800-656-4673)

4. National Runaway Safeline:
- Hotline: 1-800-RUNAWAY (1-800-786-2929)

5. GLBT National Help Center (LGBTQ+):
- Hotline: 1-888-843-4564
- Website: www.glbthotline.org

These resources are here to provide support, but if you or someone you know is in immediate danger or experiencing a crisis, please call emergency services (911) or go to the nearest emergency room. Additionally, consider reaching out to local mental health and addiction treatment centers in your area.

Compassionate Reflection

Who can you call when you are having a craving?

Ex. My sponsor, a warmline or hotline, a sober peer, a good friend, my therapist, my pastor

_____

_____

_____

_____

List any warmlines or hotlines for substance use from the list provided that you can call:

(Ex. NAMI.org, warmline.org):

_____

_____

_____

_____

Do you know about intherooms.com? Online free meetings 24/7. List meetings you can attend online or in person here:

_____

_____

_____

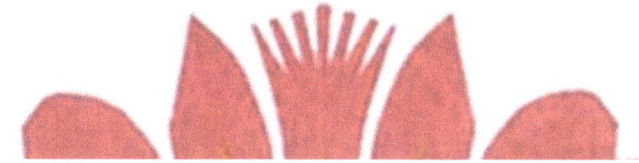

Do you know where a recovery meeting is every day of the week? You don't have to attend daily, but knowing when and where meetings are in advance is helpful. List a meeting Monday through Sunday below.

_____
_____
_____
_____
_____
_____
_____

What compassion can you offer yourself that going to a new meeting or talking to a new person can be anxiety-producing?

Ex. They've been there too. Everyone in recovery rooms remembers what it feels like to be newly sober and anxious. Everyone going through new sobriety feels uncomfortable; I'm not alone.

_____
_____
_____
_____
_____
_____
_____

What understanding or compassion can you give yourself that your cravings will continue to happen and it's not your fault?

Ex. I can learn how my addiction works. I can learn how to navigate my cravings. My cravings are not a sign of weakness; cravings just show that my addiction monster is hungry!

People often use substances to soothe themselves when life gets hard. To soothe emotions and to make life feel more manageable. Learning how to soothe yourself without substances in sobriety is an essential skill. Learning how to soothe yourself when you're craving or just having a hard day is important.

It's very uncomfortable to crave substance, and it's very painful to crave something that is destroying your life. So, you may need some soothing when experiencing this difficult time.

Take a moment and think about what calms you physically, mentally, spiritually, and emotionally. For each person, this will be different. It can be helpful to think about soothing in terms of our senses.

Thinking about smells, what smells soothe you? This may be incense, candles, lotion, or Fabuloso. Even soothing perfume or soothing cologne can help throughout the day.

Next, think about touch or texture. You could use a fuzzy or weighted blanket, your favorite sweatshirt or hoodie, the feel of grass under your feet, or your most comfortable pajamas. Think about what textures soothe you the most.

Next, think about sounds. What sounds bring you the most soothing? For a lot of people, this is music. I mentioned the benefit of healing frequencies earlier in this chapter, but any music can be soothing. *I caution you not to listen to music that you used to listen to while you were using substances because this can make a craving worse.* Maybe it would help you to listen to white noise or brown noise; you can find these sounds online; they sound a lot like a fan. Or maybe it's nature sounds or meditation music that soothes you.

Online can be a great place to type in "relaxing music, meditation music, nature sounds, healing frequencies, classical music." Online, you can find a lot of resources that can soothe you. Any music you've listened to that brings you joy, or relaxation will work for soothing.

Next, let's explore your body sensations. Somatic exercises, yoga and trauma-focused yoga, reiki, massage, tai chi qigong, and many other mindful movements can be very soothing for the body.

Take a moment to explore how you hold tension in your body and if you can release this tension. Explore releasing tension from the top of the head to the bottom of the feet. Relaxing control of the breath. Relaxing the jaw, relaxing the shoulders, and relaxing the pelvic floor.

Move or shake the body if needed. Dance. Run. Climb. The body always remembers what we have been through and often gets stuck in a fight, flight or freeze response. A way to engage in soothing the body is by tuning into its needs and allowing it rest or movement when needed.

All cravings have a beginning, a middle, and an end, so it can be important to learn these skills to manage cravings better.

Manage is the word that is key because,

You cannot avoid or prevent cravings.

They will happen because your brain has been re-wired (remember, you are a pickle!), but learning how to manage them can make recovery much easier.

Compassionate Reflection

How can you soothe your craving?

Ex. Take a hot bath, listen to healing frequencies, watch a funny movie, and call a loving friend.

Lastly, it's okay to go ahead and distract the craving. Think about hobbies or interests that you've put to the side during your addiction. Now is a great time to get those started again. Not only will these positive activities give you some pleasure-based chemicals in the brain that will make you feel happier, but they will also give your addiction some competition. Also, it will give you some time away from focusing just on your cravings and your disease.

Think about things that bring you joy, whether this is your hobbies, such as creating art, cleaning the house, cooking, spending time in nature, walking your dog, fishing, going thrifting, fixing cars, painting, playing basketball, shopping, playing sports with your children, crafting, writing or journaling, etc.

It's okay to distract yourself, but make sure you only do this *AFTER* you tell on the disease and soothe yourself. Too often, people try to distract, but they never really acknowledge what's going on and say it out loud or learn how to self-soothe in a sober way.

Acknowledging and soothing your craving first is an essential step to learn better how and why you experience cravings and what to do when they occur.

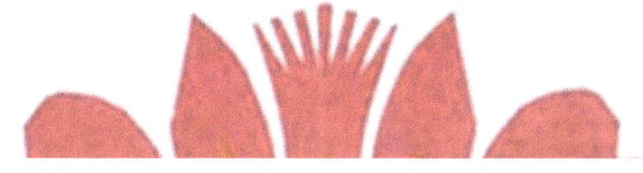

Compassionate Reflection

How can you distract your craving?

Ex. Hobbies, house cleaning, bills, calling old friends, exercising, playing with kids or pets.

Why do we want to attend to cravings? Simply because they lead to relapse. I want to introduce a concept called "relapse drift." Relapse often results from a gradual build-up of difficult emotions, increased cravings, and letting go of the things that helped to keep you sober, such as attending meetings, volunteering, or engaging in positive activities. As you let go of the things that got you sober, you start to drift closer and closer to relapse.

Relapse can be so sneaky because if you are not aware that you are suppressing emotions, ignoring cravings, or letting go of your positive and supportive activities, you will find yourself staring down the monster of addiction and heading toward relapse. Beware of relapse drift!

Compassionate Reflection

To prevent relapse drift, first, identify what is helping to keep me sober.

Ex. Meetings like AA/NA, hobbies, practicing spirituality, self-care, and self-soothing, telling on my cravings.

_____

_____

_____

_____

How do you know when you are suppressing my emotions?

Ex. My "volcano" is about to erupt; I'm irritable and snapping at everyone about dumb stuff.

_____

_____

_____

_____

How do you know when you are ignoring your cravings?

Ex. All I keep doing is thinking about the good times I had drinking.

_____

_____

_____

How can I have compassion for myself that it can be challenging at times to maintain sobriety when addiction is so tempting?

Ex. I hate that I crave cocaine more than spending time with my family, and it creates a lot of shame for me. It's okay that I crave it, but I can remember that I do love my family, and they are important to me. It's ok. I crave it because my mind has been addicted for a long time.

_____

_____

_____

_____

_____

_____

How can I have compassion for myself that staying engaged in meetings or positive activities can be exhausting if I'm not motivated to do it or it's uncomfortable for me?

Ex. It's so exhausting having social anxiety in meetings. What is nice, though, is how I don't feel alone there and often hear something that helps me. My anxiety isn't as bad as it used to be, so I have hope it may get easier over time.

_____

_____

_____

_____

_____

_____

COMPASSIONATE RETHINKING & THE 4 C's

"We don't see things as they are,
we see them as we are."

Anaïs Nin

The messages you tell yourself and the thoughts you think can significantly impact your recovery. If you find yourself being largely critical, hostile, or harsh on yourself, it can make your recovery so much more difficult.

The tool we want to learn about next is rethinking, which originates from Cognitive Behavioral Therapy (CBT). The first part of rethinking we can use is the three Cs; they stand for *Catch it, Check it, and Change it*. I like to add a **4th C,**

Catch it, Check it & Change it
with COMPASSION

So, the first part is to catch our thoughts- to recognize the thinking that we're having that is not helpful. We're not going to beat ourselves up for having automatic negative thoughts or "stinking thinking" because it's often just the thought we have thought more times than others.

Remember, our brain likes repetition, and our brain goes back to what we have done the most in the past. So, if you have told yourself the most often- "I am no good," "I'm crazy," "I'm never going to get better," "I'm never going to stay sober," etc. These are the thoughts that your brain is going to go to automatically.

We often go back to the thoughts that are connected to addiction or trauma because trauma and addiction both rewire your brain chemically and structurally.

The thoughts that are the oldest, the strongest chemically, and the most frequently used are our automatic thoughts. We don't want to beat ourselves up for automatic thoughts because this is based on repetition and the brain's wiring.

It can be overwhelming to start to examine your thinking. Your mind can sometimes even be like a bad neighborhood that you shouldn't visit alone. It's okay and often necessary to invite others into the process of exploring our thinking. Other's minds can often give a needed perspective or a change in perspective that you cannot provide yourself when doing this work alone.

Tuning into our thoughts can be a messy and challenging process initially.

I often talk about how we hear our thoughts:

Trauma and addiction scream.
Recovery whispers.
Spirituality is silent.

Trauma and addiction thoughts can sometimes sound like a scream and can be very hard to ignore or silence. Recovery can sound like a whisper and can be hard to tune into or hear. Spirituality is often silent. We often must sit quietly to better hear the voices of spirituality and recovery.

What we can do is once we recognize that these harmful or old patterns of thoughts have come up, we can decide what we want to replace those thoughts with.

This is where we catch the thought and then where we change the thought.

Rethinking is our moment of power and agency!

Compassionate Reflection

Please take a moment and think about some of the automatic thinking you struggle with that comes up most often during your day, and write it below.

Ex. I'm stupid, I'll never stay sober, I'm an old dog, and I can't learn anything new; I'm broken, I'm f*cked up.

Critical Self Talk Statement #1:

Ex. I'm never going to stay sober; I always relapse.

_____

_____

_____

Compassionate Replacement thought:

Ex. I can take it one day at a time; I can always grow and change even if it didn't happen in the past, and I can rewrite my future. It's okay and understandable if I don't feel confident; my confidence will grow over time.

_____

_____

_____

_____

_____

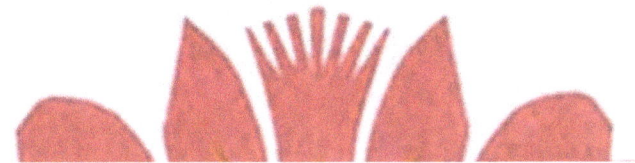

Critical Self Talk Statement #2:

Ex. I'm crazy, and drugs are the only thing that calms my racing thoughts.

_____

_____

_____

Compassionate Replacement thought:

Ex. I do have anxiety, and I may even have some undiagnosed PTSD or ADHD. Living with mental health issues is hard for everyone, and it takes a lot of support, education, and self-care to navigate the ups and downs. Drugs only complicate it and make it even harder for me.

_____

_____

_____

_____

_____

_____

_____

_____

_____

_____

_____

_____

_____

Critical Self Talk Statement #3:

Ex. I have no idea how to live sober; I'll mess this up.

_____

_____

_____

Compassionate Replacement thought:

Ex. I can slowly learn day by day who I am and what I want and need out of life. It's ok if my healing takes time. I'm worth taking care of.

_____

_____

_____

_____

_____

_____

_____

_____

_____

_____

_____

_____

_____

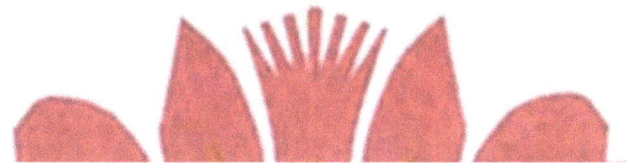

Critical Self Talk Statement #4:

"I have no idea how to be social or date sober; what kind of 40-year-old doesn't know how to go on a date?"

_____

_____

_____

Compassionate Replacement thought:

Anyone who is going through a life change, whether it be divorce, sobriety, or coming out, goes through an initial phase of not being sure of how to connect with others romantically. I can offer myself patience and move slowly as I learn what is comfortable and safe for me.

_____

_____

_____

_____

_____

_____

_____

_____

_____

_____

_____

Next, take a moment and explore a replacement thought for each of the statements that you listed above.

Remember, if you're having difficulty coming up with your compassionate replacement thoughts, it's okay to ask others what they tell themselves when having these thoughts.

A helpful tool for rethinking is to explore what you would say to a friend, a child, or someone you love if they were thinking the same as you. What kind words or understanding would you say to them if they were stuck in critical or harsh self-talk?

Always remember, it's not what we are experiencing that causes our suffering; it's what we TELL ourselves about our life circumstances that most impact us.

So, being mindful about what you say to yourself will always impact you more than what is happening around you.

Be gentle with yourself, and remember, it's not helpful to beat yourself up for this thinking; it's just a pattern you've used to survive for so many years.

Negative thinking can often be motivating when we're a child because it creates fear, and fear creates action. However, as we get older, this thinking no longer motivates us. Instead, it makes our spirit sink and leaves us less motivated.

Instead of harshness, criticism, or shame, we will lean into kindness, forgiveness, grace, inspiration, and compassion.

It will feel very different and may feel cheesy or fake, but that's okay. It's still beneficial as you learn to talk to yourself with more kindness.

THE COMFORT ZONE

"A comfort zone is a beautiful place –
but nothing ever grows there."

Unknown

I want you to take a moment and think about what your best life might look like. I want you to think about what your most healthy, most happy life would entail. What would you be doing? Who would you be spending time with? What hobbies or interests have you developed? What brings you happiness?

Now, take a moment and think about how your life was during your worst place of addiction. Think about what people surrounded you, what activities you engaged in, and how you felt most of the time.

For a lot of you, you're most healed, and happy life is what you are aiming for. Here is the catch.

You will be drawn to your comfort zone repeatedly, even if it is killing you.

You will be drawn to your comfort zone because, as we discussed, your brain has been rewired to crave these experiences. After all, they are connected chemically and structurally to your substance use.

So even though your new hobbies, activities, and friendships are in your best interest and lead to happiness and healing, you may feel uncomfortable doing these things. This doesn't mean for you not to do them, but it means to *expect discomfort* because you are now outside of your comfort zone. This involves becoming friends with discomfort and knowing that discomfort often means that you are creating new highways in your brain and developing new patterns.

Become friends with discomfort. Lean into discomfort!

Over time, these new highways and behaviors will become more comfortable, but initially, know that you will not be motivated or feel comfortable doing things that save your life or bring you joy. *Do them anyway.*

Compassionate Reflection

What do you want to do that is outside of your comfort zone?

Ex. SOBRIETY! Travel abroad, dating sober, going to AA alone.

_____

_____

_____

_____

_____

_____

What is inside of your comfort zone that is risky or harmful?

Ex. Using friends, isolation, no hobbies, just watching TV/phone/internet.

_____

_____

_____

_____

_____

_____

_____

ONE BREATH AT A TIME

"Be here now."

Ram Dass

Next, we will learn the tool of using "one breath at a time." This phrase was first introduced by author Kevin Griffin, who gave his book this name when discussing Buddhism and the 12 Steps.

Most people are familiar with the recovery, saying, "One day at a time." It is an essential slogan of many recovery meetings, so I wanted to take a moment to explore the saying. As we covered, because addiction has rewired our brains, we must learn how to, at times, psych out ourselves and psych out our monster of addiction.

Take a moment and say to your addiction, "I'm going to be sober for the rest of my life." Now listen to what it says…it will probably say something like- "Yeah, right," or "You'll be back," or it may even laugh at you.

Now, say to your addiction, "I'm not going to use it for the next five years." It's probably going to laugh at you again. Now, say to your addiction, "I'm not going to use it for the next year." It may start to say something like "Yeah, maybe," or "You'll be back," or you might feel some confidence. Now, say to your addiction, "I'm not going to use for the next month." you may start to be able to shake your head yes or say, "Yeah, maybe I can do that," and there may be an increased level of confidence.

Now, say to your addiction, "I'm not going to use it for today." What does it say? Your addiction may not have as much of a comeback to this statement. For a lot of people, you start to feel even more confidence in the ability to remain sober.

Now, we will take it even to a smaller increment of time. Now, say to yourself, "I'm not going to use it for this hour." How does that feel for any of you? *Are you feeling stronger?* You may start to feel an increased level of confidence and ability to stay sober because you know that you can withstand your addiction for one hour. It feels good.

Now tell yourself, "I'm not going to use it for this breath." How do you feel? You believe that statement, right? Addiction has nothing to say now, does it?! *It feels amazing, right?!* You feel entirely competent and able to be sober in this moment!!

That's the trick! That life is made up of nothing but small moments. Life is lived, one breath at a time.

I always remind my patients, "How do you eat a pizza? One bite at a time". 😊

When you feel that your addiction is too much to handle or that you're never going to be able to remain sober through all of life's ups and downs, bring the lens in smaller and smaller until it is a framework that feels manageable to you. For a lot of people, it's one breath at a time.

This life can be challenging, and being sober can be very difficult, but we can manage it successfully and with joy, *one breath at a time.*

Compassionate Reflection

What does your addiction say when you say you'll be sober for the rest of your life?

Ex. It just laughed at me and said, "Yeah, right, buddy".

_____

_____

_____

What does your addiction say when you say to it that you are going to be sober for the next five years?

Ex. It laughed again and said, "No, you won't".

_____

_____

_____

What does your addiction say when you say to it that you're going to be sober for the next year?

Ex. It said, "Maybe, but you'll be back."

_____

_____

_____

What does your addiction say when you're going to be sober for the next week?

Ex. *It shut up and said, "We'll see." Then I started to hear my voice too, and it said, "I bet I could do that."*

_____

_____

_____

_____

What does your addiction say when you're going to be sober for the next day?

Ex. *"I think I could do this; I can do anything for a day."*

_____

_____

_____

_____

What does your addiction say when you're going to be sober for the next hour?

Ex. *"Shoot, I'm going to be busy anyways," I may not even think about it.*

_____

_____

_____

_____

What does your addiction say? When you tell it, you're going to be sober for the next breath?

Ex. "I got this! No worries at all!"

_____

_____

_____

_____

Keep reminding yourself you've got this, one breath at a time.

THE DINSOAUR AND THE CARROT STEW:

Learning the negativity bias

"Your brain is like Velcro for negative experiences but Teflon for positive ones."

Rick Hanson

One day long ago, two of your ancestors went hunting and foraging for food. One of the ancestors who was out that day got eaten by a dinosaur, and the other ancestor ran home to find that their partner had made them some delicious carrot stew. For the ancestor that survived, which event do you think they remember more strongly? The dinosaur eating his cousin or the delicious carrot stew?

Of course, he remembered his cousin being eaten by a dinosaur more strongly!

To survive as a species, we have created the negativity bias in our brains. The negativity bias was first documented by psychologists Paul Rozin and Edward Royzman.

The negativity bias describes that the experiences we tend to remember the most strongly in the brain are the most negative or traumatic. This is a survival mechanism. We want to remember the things that can harm us so that we can avoid them in the future and survive.

However, the problem is that the things that make us happy, bring us joy or subtle pleasure sometimes get skipped over because we're preoccupied with the negative.

Many people can experience this as always thinking about what could go wrong or remembering the negative things they did but not the positive.

Many people define themselves out of the worst things they've done while forgetting the multitudes of positive, kind, or loving things they have done in their lifetimes.

One exercise to strengthen our ability to see the positive or to feel happiness is when we experience joy, happiness, or pleasure to sit with it for 5-10 seconds and take in all the sensory experiences of that moment. How does it feel in your mind/body/spirit?

What about that moment is bringing you happiness? Just sit with it, describe the moment, resonate with it, and allow the brain to make the connection that *this thing makes me happy*. Over time, what will happen is your brain will start to make associations that this thing makes you happy, and when you see this thing, you will feel happiness.

You still will notice the negative, you still will be drawn to the negative, but you will also be drawn to the positive and the happy. The goal is to rewire our brains to have a wider lens. Expand our lens to experience both the negative, the neutral, and the positive. Our goal is to experience the sadness, the neutral and the joy and not be predisposed to one over the other.

Happiness takes bravery. Happiness can sometimes be a choice. Happiness is most definitely a practice.

The happiness practice becomes noticing when you are happy and taking a moment to savor it, to understand it, and to sit with it so that you can be better predisposed to experience more happiness in the future.

Compassionate Reflection

What makes you happy?

Ex. My kids are eating pasta, my dog wagging its tail when my team wins, and my cousin's jokes.

_____

_____

_____

_____

_____

_____

Choose one thing that makes you happy and describe it in detail. Describe where you feel happiness in the body.

Ex. It's the way my dog is always happy to see me after a long day at work, with her cute face and her happy tail. I always feel so loved when I look at her, and for a moment, everything feels okay. When I see her, my heart feels more love, my belly and breath relax and I smile.

_____

_____

_____

_____

_____

_____

What negative things (memories, thoughts, images) do you frequently reference or fall prey to?

Ex. I'm always thinking about what I've done wrong, but I never explore what I've done right. I know all my mistakes, but I never look at my successes; I want to spend more time looking at what I've done right.

LOOK FOR THE GLIMMERS

"If you happen to see something beautiful,
do not hesitate to call it by its name."

Joél Leon

Most people are familiar with the term trigger, which means something that activates you. In addiction, a lot of your triggers to use substances are going to be reminders of the people, places, and things associated with substance use.

However, triggers can also be our emotional experiences or even our trauma history and can be a trigger for PTSD symptoms or an increased emotional intensity.

For each of you, what triggers a craving or desire to use a substance or activates your emotions will be different because each of us is a uniquely different person.

What I would like to introduce is the concept of the glimmer. A glimmer is the opposite of a trigger. It's a concept coined by Deb Dana LCSW. A glimmer is anything that brings you joy, happiness, and peace; paying attention to them as they come through your day is important. Glimmers refers to small moments in our lives when our biology is in a place of connection or regulation, which then cues our nervous system to feel safe or calm.

Noticing glimmers will activate the neural networks of happiness in the brain when we purposefully pay attention to them. So, as you move through your day, no matter how little or how mundane, if this glimmer brings you joy, peace, happiness, or calm, if you giggle, take note of it and pay attention to it.

The magic is, once you practice this, you'll notice these glimmers more and more! Remember, there is no glimmer too small. If the smell of laundry detergent makes you happy, that's a glimmer! If the way your cat purrs makes you happy, that's a glimmer! When a stranger says hello to you and means it, that's a glimmer! If the way the clouds move across the sky brings you peace, that's a glimmer!

It will be different for each of us, but it's so important and powerful to notice these things because, again, life is full of triggers, but life is also full of glimmers.

Remember that there are glimmers in your life today that you once wished and prayed for. You must continue to notice these glimmers and explore them. Or else, happiness becomes an ever-moving goalpost of "I'll be happy when…". You will never feel happy if you never take the time actually to notice that you're happy at the moment.

Notice the happiness, gratitude, well-being, and calm while it is here; the present moment is all we have!

Compassionate Reflection

What glimmers have you experienced this week?

Ex. The way my dog looks at me, thunderstorms, this fantastic pizza I had, laughing at a meme.

_____
_____
_____
_____
_____
_____
_____

What glimmers bring you the most happiness, peace, or joy?

Ex. Being outside in nature, when my team wins, when my kids tell me they love me.

_____
_____
_____
_____
_____
_____
_____

WHAT COULD GO RIGHT?

"I survived because the fire that burned inside of me burned brighter than the fire around me."

Unknown

There is a huge connection between trauma and substance use. So much so that I think an entire additional workbook needs to be made regarding how to heal from trauma compassionately (it's next on the list!). I would be amiss If I didn't add something about Post-Traumatic Stress Disorder (PTSD) and trauma to this workbook.

Before we explore trauma's role in rewiring the brain, it's important to understand the role of the autonomic nervous system.

The sympathetic and parasympathetic nervous systems are two branches of the autonomic nervous system, and they play complementary roles in working to regulate various bodily functions.

The sympathetic nervous system prepares the body for action and responds to stress. In contrast, the parasympathetic nervous system facilitates rest, recovery, and normal bodily functions during times of relaxation. These two systems work in balance to adapt to the body's varying needs depending on the situation.

What happens for many people is they get stuck in the stress response, the sympathetic nervous system, due to their trauma.

Why is this?

Trauma also rewires the brain. Trauma creates a shortcut in the brain between your trauma and anything that reminds you of the trauma. So, when these reminders are activated, the brain lights up with adrenaline and cortisol and says, "It's time to survive." The body then goes into the limited choices of, I need to fight, I need to flight, I need to freeze, I need to fawn (people pleasing). The brain says, my only choices are to survive, and this is what I need to do to survive.

This is where substance use comes in because when you're in a fight or flight response for a long time, it's hugely uncomfortable. You have insomnia, you're irritable, you jump and or startle easily, you have nightmares, you engage in worst-case scenario thinking, you have thoughts about the trauma that come to you without your permission, and then you start to change the way you think about yourself and the world.

Living with trauma is hugely uncomfortable, and so a lot of people turn to substances to cope with these very uncomfortable symptoms. This makes sense because it works. Substance use works to relieve the symptoms of trauma. However, the trick is that once you sober up, the levels jump right back up, and you're just as uncomfortable as you were before, except now you also have an addiction on top of trauma.

The key is to learn how to manage your trauma symptoms without addiction. First, it's essential to learn about PTSD and how it impacts the body. PTSD is a stress disorder, and it works with stress hormones. So, if we learn about what stress is, we can learn to work with our PTSD or fight against it by reducing our stress.

Not all stress is bad. We need stress to survive, to be able to respond quickly in traffic, to be able to run quickly if a dog is chasing us, etc. We don't want to eliminate our stress response because it keeps us alive.

However, the problem is when you have an increased stress response when there is no threat. When you're sitting at home, and you're in an environment with safe people, you still feel unsafe. This is when you can use the skills of learning to reduce your stress hormones so that when you are in a safe environment, you feel safe. When you are loved, you feel loved. The goal is for you to be able to align your external reality with your internal reality.

I often tell people I need you to chill out as if your life depends on it. Many people think stress reduction is an extravagance, but it's necessary and can make you live longer. Exposure to chronic stress leads to the most common causes of death, in America specifically.

Think about anything that calms you down, chills you out, or de-stresses you. Maybe this is time in nature, music, gardening or watering your house plants, spending time with your animals or your children, getting a hug from your partner, yoga, watching football, organizing your house or cleaning your home, playing an instrument, going to thrift stores, and the list goes on and on…

Please take a moment and explore the things that relax or chill you out. Make a list of those activities, and I need you to practice them *every day* if you have symptoms of stress or PTSD.

Compassionate Reflection

What are activities that reduce my stress:

Ex. Hot bath, burning incense, walking outside, meditation, music, exercise.

Because of stress and trauma, as well as the negativity bias that we discussed previously, your brains will often tell you or prepare you for *what could go wrong*, so much so that you spend a lot of your time focused on potential threats in the future.

You devise every scenario of what could go wrong in the future, and what does it do? It increases your stress hormones in the present. Conversely, when you think about the past, and you think about all the things that you have done wrong, it increases your depression or stress hormones.

The body does not know when the mind has time traveled. The body responds chemically to where the mind goes.

The key is to stay in the present moment as much as possible. You can visit the past in therapy or journaling; going there purposefully is okay. You can go to the future and make plans, schedule your life, and make a vision board or a list of your goals, and that's great.

But what you want to watch out for is letting your mind wander aimlessly between past regrets and future worries. Ultimately, what you will feel like is a ping pong ball going back and forth between depression, anxiety, depression, anxiety, depression, anxiety, and with lots and lots of stress hormones.

One helpful skill is when the brain starts to say what could go wrong, ask yourself.

What could go right?

What could go right?? *Now, hold space for both.* It's okay to still plan for the worst-case scenario, but preparing for the best-case scenario is important because each is just as likely as the other.

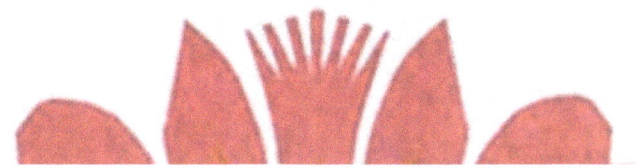

Compassionate Reflection

Homework ideas:

1. Watch or read "Good News" instead of the traditional bad news. Or watch or read both to give yourself a full perspective. But remember, we as a species were not designed to hear about the suffering of ALL beings around the ENTIRE globe in REAL TIME. So, be mindful of what you feed your brain and heart regularly.

2. Read about the concept of "post-traumatic growth." This is the idea that there can be growth and even gifts from suffering and healing from trauma. You may not have wanted or deserved the trauma, but this does not mean that because of the trauma, you have not evolved specific skills, insights, and personality traits that allow you not only to heal but to thrive in the face of adversity!

Compassionate Reflection

What worst-case scenario messages do I tell myself?

Ex. I'm never going to be sober; I'm always going to be crazy; I'm not safe anywhere; I'm always waiting for the other shoe to drop.

_____

_____

_____

_____

_____

Looking at these examples, explore the other side; what could go right?

Ex. I can be sober for this week and grow my sobriety day by day. I may always have some mental health challenges, but I can heal over time; I'm safe in my home most of the time.

_____

_____

_____

_____

_____

_____

CLEANING THE WOUND

"A journey of a thousand miles
begins with a single step."

Lao Tzu

A lot of you have been addicted or experiencing symptoms of trauma for many years, and I like to think of this process as cleaning a wound. You've had this one for many years. It's largely infected and uncomfortable, taking up all your brain space daily. All you can do is think about this wound. You look at it, but you don't do anything about it.

Well, now you're doing something about it! Think about what happens when you first clean out a wound. It's super painful, it's super uncomfortable, and it's very tender. That's what you're doing right now. Initially, this experience will be very painful and tender, and you'll need help and support to clean out this wound, and that's okay.

Then think about what happens over time… it starts to heal. It starts to become less tender, and eventually, with love, care, and support, it heals completely. But it's a process.

Healing is a process that takes time, constant care, and attention, and you are no different. Have patience with yourself as you heal, and know that initially, when you start to feel the emotions that you've pushed away when you begin to be honest with yourself about the condition of your life and how addiction has affected you, you're going to feel very tender, and this may be very painful for some people.

The initial cleaning of the wound may feel like a wave of emotion, like a tidal wave that washes over you, and you feel like you're going to drown.

Please believe me; your head will be above water after that initial surge of emotion, pain, and tenderness. You will continue to have waves of suffering and sadness and pain, but your head will be above water, and you will learn to manage and cope with your newly felt emotions instead of suppressing them or allowing them to consume you.

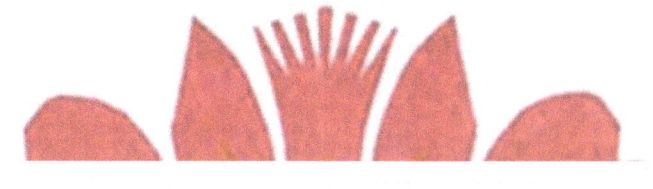

Compassionate Reflection

What words of kindness do I need when I am feeling emotionally overwhelmed?

Ex. Everyone sometimes gets emotionally overwhelmed; this life is no joke. It's okay for me to sit with what I'm feeling and investigate it a little, then offer myself some love.

_____

_____

_____

_____

_____

_____

What do I need from myself and others when I feel tender, emotionally vulnerable, or scared of the healing process?

Ex. I need a hug and someone to tell me I don't have to do this life alone.

_____

_____

_____

_____

_____

_____

SELF-FORGIVENESS

"Our feelings are our most genuine
paths to knowledge."

Audre Lorde

When starting the journey of self-forgiveness, it can be very important to tease out the difference between guilt and shame. Shame is a focus that I *am* as a person who is somehow flawed, a mistake, or a bad person. Guilt suggests that something I *did* is somehow flawed, a mistake, or bad.

You cannot do anything with shame. Shame causes you to shut down, isolate yourself, not speak about your experiences, and can result in a negative view of yourself. This negative view of self can sometimes cause you to engage in self-destructive behaviors or avoid your emotional experiences altogether.

When you stay stuck in shame, it often takes away from your self-esteem and makes it very difficult to engage in a path of recovery. Simply because you feel you are not worthy or capable of healing and recovery.

Guilt, however, is something that you can work with. Guilt does not mean that what you did was okay or that what you did was not a mistake.

Guilt can be helpful because it lets you know that your actions go against your moral compass or values.

So, having guilt isn't necessarily a negative thing, although it can feel like a negative experience for people. Guilt gives you information that this is an area of healing for you.

When you work with guilt, you can first identify what it is that you feel guilty about. Next, you can explore what additional emotions come up when I feel guilty. What emotions are present for me when I think about this event for which I hold so much guilt? Next, you can meet our guilt with self-compassion. Lastly, you can work on making amends for what you did. If you're involved in step work, you'll recognize making amends as one of the steps in recovery.

You are worthy of forgiveness. Others may not forgive all your actions, but you are worthy of forgiveness for being imperfect, growing, and learning. This is a powerful distinction.

What are some ways that you can show yourself forgiveness? What are some ways that you can show yourself kindness for the mistakes you made during your healing journey?

Self-forgiveness is a lot like self-care. It is believing that you are worthy of caring for your mind, body, and spirit. Self-forgiveness can look like working with your guilt and bringing it to light. Self-forgiveness can look like offering yourself compassion over complex emotions you have when you think about the mistakes you have made in your life or addictions.

Compassionate Reflection

Have you felt shame and thought, "I am a bad person." Put into words how you have experienced shame.

Ex. I can't even talk about what I have shame over, but I'll try. I'm so embarrassed about the way I treated people in my addiction; it's like I'm a different person. And I hate the person I become when I'm drinking. The shame makes me want to drink more. I've never told anyone about how much shame I have over my past mistakes.

_____

_____

_____

_____

_____

_____

_____

_____

_____

_____

_____

_____

_____

_____

_____

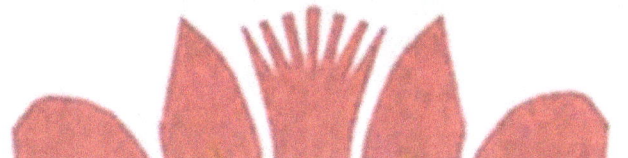

What is it that I feel guilty about?

Ex. Not being there for my kids, disconnecting from people who love me, cussing out people who didn't deserve it.

_____
_____
_____
_____
_____
_____
_____

What emotions come up when I feel guilty? What emotions are present for me when I think about this event for which I hold so much guilt?

Ex. Guilt, shame, remorse, embarrassment, sadness, fear, anxiety, hopelessness

_____
_____
_____
_____
_____
_____
_____

How can I meet my guilt with self-compassion? What words of kindness would I offer a friend who made the same mistakes?

Ex. The only way we learn is by making mistakes. The real shame would be if I didn't learn from this. At least now, I know what not to do, which can help me understand what I need to do. I'd tell a friend that it's not okay to yell at others when you're drunk and to get help for addiction. I'd say to them everyone has made mistakes and that they can learn from their mistakes and change their behaviors in the future.

_____

_____

_____

_____

_____

_____

Lastly, how can you make amends if you hurt someone else?

Ideas: Write them a letter (even if you don't send it); donate to a cause associated with the event; volunteer with others who are less fortunate; say "I'm sorry" to those you have harmed; work with a sponsor on making amends.

_____

_____

_____

_____

_____

_____

IT TAKES A VILLAGE

"A human being is part of a whole, called by us the 'Universe' —a part limited in time and space. He experiences himself, his thoughts, and feelings, as something separated from the rest—a kind of optical delusion of his consciousness. This delusion is a kind of prison for us, restricting us to our personal desires and to affection for a few persons nearest us. Our task must be to free ourselves from this prison by widening our circles of compassion to embrace all living creatures and the whole of nature in its beauty."

Albert Einstein

Addiction thrives in isolation. Often, when someone is experiencing addiction or even mental health diagnoses, isolation can become very commonplace. Isolation activates the pain centers in your brain and contributes to your mental health deteriorating.

Part of recovery that can be very helpful is reconnecting with others. This is partially why meetings like AA or NA can be very healing for people because they find a community where they are understood and feel safe.

Reconnecting to any community, whether it be the recovery community, a spiritual community, a volunteer community, a military community, or a family, can become essential to long-term recovery. Connecting to others allows you to develop sober relationships, engage in positive activities, and explore life outside your comfort zone.

Connecting to people is easier said than done. It can be hard to find places to meet new friends; it can be hard to repair relationships with those who have hurt during your addiction.

Mental health diagnoses, such as anxiety or depression, can make it difficult to connect to or start conversations with new people. Having compassion for yourself as you navigate creating new relationships or repairing old ones is essential. Let's start first with forming new relationships.

With new relationships and recovery, I give you permission to make it awkward. It's okay if there is an awkward silence, you say the wrong thing, and you're "weird."

Surprise, we are all weird 😊 It would be massively boring if we were all the same.

Give yourself permission to make it awkward because, guess what? Everybody is doing their best, and there will be people out there who will be your people, who will not care whether you are awkward, strange, or weird. They will revel in it and love you because of it. Why? Because you are their people.

However, there is a risk in this because some people will reject you, which can be hard to deal with. That doesn't mean to stop trying! I promise there will be people who will love your sober version and understand your healing version. Just don't stop looking…

Compassionate Reflection

What is the hardest part for you about meeting new people?

Ex. I'm so anxious and awkward! I never know what to say, and silence makes me want to run! Where do adults even meet new friends?

_____

_____

_____

_____

What places can you go to find new friendships?

Ex. meetup.com, AA/NA, hobbies you enjoy, the gym, spiritual places.

_____

_____

_____

_____

What compassion can you offer yourself for the parts of you that are awkward, aka unique?

Ex. I have much to offer and come out of my shell once I get comfortable.

_____

_____

_____

IT'S NOT ALL ABOUT YOU

(Even though you are pretty amazing!)

"To love. To be loved. To never forget your own insignificance. To never get used to the unspeakable violence and the vulgar disparity of life around you. To seek joy in the saddest places. To pursue beauty to its lair. To never simplify what is complicated or complicate what is simple. To respect strength, never power. Above all, to watch. To try and understand. To never look away. And never, never to forget."

Arundhati Roy

The title is harsh, huh? But addiction can be very self-focused, and one tool of recovery that can be very helpful is to not make it all about you all of the time. To get out of your bubble and help those more vulnerable than you.

This skill can be very inspiring and rewarding. Whether volunteering at your local dog shelter, going to a local garden and helping them till the soil, or feeding those experiencing homelessness, it can be very rewarding to contribute to the well-being of others and work to reduce their suffering.

I find it very interesting that by helping to relieve the suffering of others, we relieve the suffering within ourselves.

You can also just get connected with people in your lives that you have let go to the wayside during addiction.

It doesn't always have to be people who are suffering. It can be that you spend more time with your child playing catch than you used to. It can be something like cooking dinner for your spouse unexpectedly just because you know they had a long day. It can be doing the laundry just because. It can be helping your neighbor mow the lawn if you know they are elderly and have difficulty.

The opportunities to get connected and show compassion to others are endless; I promise you it will be worth it.

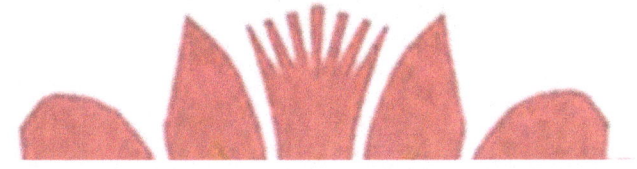

Compassionate Reflection

What can you do to help someone or something that is suffering?

Ex. I've thought about volunteering at the homeless shelter; I can give money to people on the street or give them food; I can volunteer at the animal shelter where they always need people; I can do a river clean-up for Earth Day.

_____

_____

_____

_____

_____

How does it feel when you help others?

Ex. I feel like I'm decent, which feels good and relieving. I remember that even though I'm going through a hard time, I'm not alone, and some people have it worse off than me. I feel great when I help someone, and they smile back at me, and I know they are grateful.

_____

_____

_____

_____

_____

To whom in your life can you show unexpected kindness? What can you do for them?

Ex. Maybe I'll take my mom out for dinner just because. I could buy my kid that game he wants and make a scavenger hunt, and it can be the final prize. I could start cooking dinner on Fridays or buy pizza to give my wife a break.

_____

_____

_____

_____

_____

_____

_____

_____

_____

_____

_____

_____

_____

_____

_____

_____

_____

_____

WE ARE ALL
A WORK IN PROGRESS

"Obstacles do not block the path; they are the path."

Anonymous

You are not broken. You do not need to be fixed. You are a work in progress; we all are. We are all on a continual path of compassionate self-realization, discovery, and healing.

We will not reach a finished product where we say, "Ah! I figured out the key to how to be a perfect human"! Each of us is on a journey of learning and understanding how to best care for ourselves and find happiness in a world of suffering.

Just know that up until your last breath, you will be a work in progress. What we are learning through the process of recovery is how to manage life's ups and downs with as much grace, self-compassion, and happiness as possible.

The goal is to avoid fixing yourself or trying to reach perfection.

The goal is to meet your imperfections with compassion, grace, kindness, and understanding and learn how to manage and sit with the discomfort of suffering when it arises.

Please remember that *you are the expert in your own life*. Only you have the answers on how to heal YOU best because you understand your life experience, your triggers, your glimmers, what activates your cravings and what causes you a desire to use, what makes you cry, what makes you happy, what activates your trauma, etc. You know this better than anyone else, so *please trust your wisdom*. You are the expert in your own life.

The more honest you become with yourself about your experiences, the more internal wisdom arises that will guide you in managing your own experience. This takes being willing to be still and to be silent, to be honest, and to be reflective on what is going on inside of you.

I promise that you are wiser and more capable of engaging in your healing than you ever thought possible.

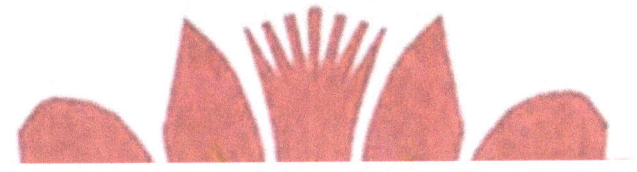

Compassionate Reflection

What reminder can you offer yourself that you are perfectly imperfect? That you are a work in progress, just like anyone else?

Ex. No one is perfect. We are all doing the best with what we have. I can always make changes one day at a time. I am capable of healing slowly and compassionately. I'm worth taking care of and allowing myself some grace as I move through this. I've got this!!

"Do not believe in anything simply because you have heard it. Do not believe in anything simply because it is spoken and rumored by many. Do not believe in anything simply because it is found written in your religious books. Do not believe in anything merely on the authority of your teachers and elders. Do not believe in traditions because they have been handed down for many generations. But after observation and analysis, when you find that anything agrees with reason and is conducive to the good and benefit of one and all, then accept it and live up to it."

Buddha

ABOUT THE AUTHOR

 **Nichole Sloan** (Nickie) is a Licensed Clinical Social Worker (LCSW), a certified Cognitively Based Compassion Training (CBCT)® teacher, and a Veteran's Administration (VA) CALM Mindfulness teacher with over 20 years of practice in the field of social work. She has extensive experience in Cognitive Behavioral Therapy (CBT), Cognitive Processing Therapy (CPT), and Mindfulness-Based Relapse Prevention.

The focus of her professional practice is on the intersection of addiction, housing insecurity, and trauma. She maintains a strong focus on integrating contemplative practices such as Mindfulness and Compassion interventions into mental health care.

Nickie enjoys time in nature, traveling, political and community activism, rescuing animals, creating art, going to festivals, decorating her home, and gardening. She practices mindfulness and compassion meditations and has a strong interest in the metaphysical and spiritual world.